D1142915

LEARNING FROM
RESEARCH

LEARNING FROM RESEARCH

Getting more from your data

JUDITH BELL
and CLIVE OPIE

Open University Press
Buckingham · Philadelphia

Open University Press
Celtic Court
22 Ballmoor
Buckingham
MK18 1XW

email: enquiries@openup.co.uk
world wide web: www.openup.co.uk

and

325 Chestnut Street
Philadelphia, PA 19106, USA

First Published 2002

Copyright © Judith Bell and Clive Opie, 2002

A catalogue record of this book is available from the British Library

ISBN   0 335 20660 3 (pb)   0 335 20661 1 (hb)

Library of Congress Cataloging-in-Publication Data
Bell, Judith, 1930–
   Learning from research: getting more from data / Judith Bell and
Clive Opie
      p. cm.
   Includes bibliographical references and index.
   ISBN 0–335–20661–1 – ISBN 0–335–20660–3 (pbk.)
   1. Dissertations, Academic–Handbooks, manuals, etc. 2. Research–
Handbooks, manuals, etc. 3. Report writing–Handbooks, manuals, etc.
I. Opie, Clive, 1953– II. Title.
LB2369 .B345 2002
808′.042–dc21   2001058070

Typeset by Graphicraft Limited, Hong Kong
Printed in Great Britain by St Edmundsbury Press Limited,
Bury St Edmunds, Suffolk

For
Helen, Gilbert, Cher Ping, Jan and Tim

CONTENTS

LIST OF FIGURES
AND TABLES

Figures

Tables

ACKNOWLEDGEMENTS

We are extremely grateful to Sandy Goulding who meticulously proof read all our drafts, queried and corrected some of our statistical misinterpretations and made many useful suggestions for alternative and better approaches. We could not have managed without her.

Our thanks also to many good friends and colleagues who happened to call for a social cup of coffee and found instead that they were press ganged into reading a draft or two rather than engaging in friendly chat. We owe many people many dinners.

Any mistakes which remain are, of course, our responsibility.

Obviously this book could not have been written without the collaboration of Helen, Gilbert, Cher Ping, Jan and Tim who generously agreed to share their good and less good research experiences with us. They all read and commented on drafts, made suggestions for additions, omissions or changes and agreed to give interviews in order to respond to our numerous queries. We took account of all their comments and made all the changes they requested. I hope they think we have done justice to their work.

Judith Bell
Clive Opie

INTRODUCTION

This book is an account of the experiences of five postgraduate research students, Helen, Gilbert, Cher Ping, Ian and Tim on their journeys to successful completion of Master of Education or PhD degrees. They share a number of characteristics, not least the fact that they all had a formidable capacity for hard work, a determination to succeed and to reach the standard required for the award of their degree in the required timescale. They knew the research would involve a major commitment of time and, in most cases, money but had decided they were prepared to commit themselves to the work in order to be able to explore their topics, which were of importance to them personally and professionally.

Their preparation for the research was admirable. They spent time locating, studying and analysing the published literature relating to their topic, wrote up as much as they could as they went along and spent what must have seemed to them to be an inordinate amount of time refining research questions, objectives and hypotheses. They tried out their ideas with colleagues, students and supervisory tutors and their data-collecting instruments went through many drafts before they were satisfied. They did not get everything right all the time but they made real efforts to eliminate faulty design and unsatisfactory wording.

Four of the investigations are mainly quantitative and one is mainly qualitative. They increase in length, depth and complexity from the descriptive study we consider in Part 1 of the book, through Parts 2 and 3 to the final doctoral investigations discussed in Parts 4 and 5. As you will see, although they are all very different, the planning and preparation processes involved are largely the same for each.

Jan already had a MEd degree before embarking on her doctoral studies and Tim had a Masters degree in auditing, though he claimed to be a rookie as far as educational research was concerned. Helen, Gilbert and Cher Ping were genuine first-time researchers. Cher Ping was the only one of the three who had a sound information technology and statistics background, which certainly helped, but he too was new to educational research. Helen claimed she knew nothing about and would not be capable of coping with even the most basic statistics in her investigation, though in fact she made use of a number of descriptive statistics. Gilbert said he was 'scared of stats' but learnt by attending a course, reading books, consulting friends colleagues and his supervisor – and by trial and error. That enabled him to be fairly confident about using various statistical tests which greatly enhanced his findings.

It is easy to become convinced that statistics, computers and statistical packages are what research is all about. It is not. They are wonderful tools as long as we know how to use them for our particular purposes, but in fact research is, and always has been, about identifying a topic that is worth investigating. It is about planning and designing a suitable methodology, designing research instruments, negotiating access to institutions, materials and people. It may involve learning new skills and techniques in order to get the most out of our data. It may or may not require a degree of statistical expertise, but without this careful planning and piloting, no amount of statistical wizardry will save us.

This was never intended to be a book about statistics. There are already many good books on the market and we provide references to a selection of them in the 'Further reading' sections at the end of each of the five Parts. Key topics are highlighted in **bold** in the main text and additional explanations of some of these (highlighted in ***bold italics***) are provided in the glossary.

Inevitably, we have only been able to select a very small part of each investigation for discussion. Some of the researchers may have felt sorry that we only had the space to select small parts of their dissertations and theses for comment. They read and commented on all drafts and if they were disappointed, they were kind enough not to object to our selections, nor to the way we simplified the language of some of their more complex items. We firmly believe that there is rarely anything which is so complex that it cannot be explained in plain language and so we have done our best to keep to that principle. We make no apologies for providing explanations of what may seem to some sophisticated readers to be stating (and regularly repeating) the obvious. What is obvious to one person is sometimes incomprehensible to another.

Our five researchers were perhaps fortunate in having experienced supervisors who responded quickly to requests for help, were not averse to laying down the law from time to time but nevertheless provided sound guidance and encouragement throughout the three, four or five years of research. Even so, they occasionally experienced periods of depression when nothing seemed to go right and when they had to cope with setbacks, many of which were not their fault. They learnt from their experiences, as we all do, emerged only a little bruised from some of the difficult times but eventually all produced dissertations and theses of real quality.

It was not all plain sailing for them, as you will see when you read about their research and their views of the experience after it was all over. All faced sharp learning curves at various times but they succeeded, and we hope their success will serve as an encouragement to anyone who might still feel anxious about undertaking a major piece of research.

● Part 1

THE DESCRIPTIVE STUDY

Background to the study and critics of descriptive studies • difference between descriptive and inferential statistics • the topic • key issues • hypotheses • piloting • hitches • questionnaires • selection of variables • question types • using computer statistical packages • preparing data for the computer • codes and coding • measurement • nominal scales • recording and summary sheets • trial analyses • keeping records and recording sources.

1.1

BACKGROUND TO THE STUDY and CRITICS OF DESCRIPTIVE STUDIES

The first study to be considered here is a Master of Education (MEd) dissertation, produced by Helen Stoneley who at the time of the research was a lecturer in Occupational Therapy (OT) in a British university (Stoneley 1995). She had not undertaken any major research before and she made it clear to her supervisor that she would not be competent to cope with complex or, she claimed, even simple statistics. However, she hoped that the use of appropriate statistical computer packages would help to remedy that deficiency. There was just one problem, which was that she had never owned or used a computer before. A computer was duly purchased, software installed and then began the process of learning how to make it all work. All that took far longer and was far more frustrating than could have been imagined. Computer manuals were incomprehensible, the original software proved to be unsatisfactory, new software had to be purchased and the whole learning process went on and on.

She quickly came to appreciate what she did not know and at first that seemed to be a great deal. She found she had to read widely, learn new techniques, try to get to grips with the mysteries of computer packages and change her mind about the progress of the research when barriers were put in her way. She made mistakes (don't we all?) but learnt from them and in the end produced a successful dissertation.

We are frequently told that just about everybody in the world, and particularly in the academic world, is computer competent, but in our experience that is not so. There's many a senior university academic who still has to learn how to switch on a computer, let alone use it. Of course, that is no consolation to a new researcher who has no secretarial or research assistant support and is about to carry out a quantitative study. As far as Helen was concerned, she had no choice. She had to get to grips with the computer, to show it who was boss and become competent enough to take advantage of its marvellous tools. It was only when she felt she had reached, or almost reached, that stage that she felt she could move on.

The topic

There is little point in embarking on a demanding piece of research that has been selected on the lines of 'couldn't think of anything else to do'. In fact it's likely to be disastrous because boredom inevitably sets in, a dozen other and better topics would no doubt have emerged if only you'd given the matter more thought before diving in to the research pool, and friends and family will become weary of hearing you moaning that it's all a waste of time and you wish you'd never started the dratted thing.

Helen did not fall into this trap. She had clearly identified an area of concern in her job which she felt should be investigated. At one time, OTs were qualified to practise after successfully completing a Diploma in OT, but the qualification had been upgraded to the degree of BSc (Hons). Significantly more students applied for the new undergraduate programme than could be accepted, and so entry qualifications were raised. Her experience made her question whether the higher entry qualifications were justified, other than as a means of rationing a small number of places. Her hunch was that they were not and she was concerned that some potentially excellent therapists might well be excluded under the new regime. However, she had no proof and decided to make the search for proof the basis for her research. That, she decided, would require a fact-finding, descriptive study.

Critics of descriptive studies

Critics of **descriptive studies** claim that description without explanation is of little value but it is our view that a case can be made for purely descriptive studies *in appropriate contexts*. Punch (1998) makes clear that description and explanation represent two different levels of understanding, description being at the basic level and explanation requiring firm evidence and, in most cases greater statistical sophistication.

> To describe is to draw a picture of what happened, or of how things are proceeding, or of what a situation of a person or an event is like . . . To explain, on the other hand, is to account for what happened, or for how things are proceeding, or for what something or someone is like . . . It involves finding the reasons for things, events and situations, showing why and how they have come to be what they are.
>
> (Punch 1998: 15)

Helen was only interested in the 'what'. Investigating the 'why' would have required more and different data, a larger and more complex investigation than she could deal with in the dissertation and the use of *inferential statistics*. Before we continue, we'd better be sure we all understand the difference between the two. Goulding explains:

> There are two broad categories into which statistical methods fall: *descriptive* and *inferential*. Descriptive statistical methods provide 'pictures' of the group under investigation: these 'pictures' may be in the form of charts, tables, percentages, averages and so on. Inferential statistical methods have a quite different purpose; they may involve the use of descriptive statistics, but their prime aim is to draw implications from the data with regard to a theory, model or body of knowledge.
>
> (Goulding 1987: 103)

In Goulding's view, the pictures presented by most small-scale studies, including Helen's, are therefore likely to be *illuminative* rather than *generalizable* – and there is nothing wrong with pictures and illumination as long as more is not claimed from the data.

1.2

THE PREPARATION

The sample and the timing

The investigation covered the three-year period for one cohort of students from their entry to the course to their final degree results. It has to be remembered that the MEd dissertation was a *partial* requirement for the degree, following on from success-ful completion of assessed work, and so selection of this one cohort of 87 students (reduced to 79 after eight students with-drew) was perfectly adequate. In fact many good dissertations and even PhD theses have had much smaller samples. In an effort to do a really thorough job, there is sometimes a tendency for researchers to take on more than they can possibly hope to complete in the time allowed, which for part-time Masters degrees is usually about one academic year and for full-time students little more than three months. Many part-time post-graduate researchers also have a job, family or other responsib-ilities. As there is a limit to the number of hours available in any one day, week or month, common sense has to prevail. The research has to be thorough and well produced, but there is no point in attempting to do enough research for a PhD or to pro-duce the definitive book on your topic if that means you never submit your dissertation.

If Helen had decided to take a sample from a much larger student population she would have had to decide on a suitable method of drawing a sample, but in this case it was not necessary or possible. Only one cohort of students operating on the new degree regulations had graduated at the time of the research. Anyone who is restricted to a specific time or a topic involving a specific population has to take what is available, subject always to the agreement of supervisors, conformity to institutional regulations and informed agreement about access.

The search for key issues

She knew from the outset what she wanted to investigate in general terms, but moving from the general to the specific required careful thought and preparation. She began by carrying out a study of the literature relating to the management of descriptive studies, student performance, and a study of documents which included university minutes of meetings, reports and policy statements relating to entry qualifications. That enabled her to identify key issues and to inform herself about university admission policies and procedures. It was only then that she felt she knew sufficiently clearly what information was needed. She decided she would need to:

- examine students' entry qualifications as contained in the university's admissions records;
- design and distribute a questionnaire to each member of the first cohort of students who were due to graduate in the year of the research which would request a variety of information about background and previous experience;
- carry out follow-up interviews with a selection of students; and
- compare students' entry qualifications with final degree results and fieldwork assessments.

All very straightforward and reasonable. Helen also decided to devise a hypothesis as a guide to her research, which stated:

Higher entry qualifications do not necessarily mean that the students will achieve a higher academic qualification.

The *hypothesis*

Before we continue, we'd better consider what a hypothesis is and what it does. Verma and Beard describe it as

> a tentative proposition which is subject to verification through subsequent investigation ... In many cases hypotheses are hunches that the researcher has about the existence of relationship between variables.
>
> (Verma and Beard 1981: 184)

Medawar develops the definition as being

> a speculative adventure, an imaginative preconception *of what might be true* – a preconception which always, and necessarily, goes a little way (sometimes a long way) beyond anything which we have logical or factual authority to believe in ... [it is] a dialogue between two voices, the one imaginative and the other critical; a dialogue, if you like, between the possible and the actual, between proposal and disposal, conjecture and criticism, between what might be true and what is in fact the case.
>
> (Medawar 1972: 22)

So, hypotheses make statements about the relationship between variables, which in Helen's case were students' entry qualifications and final degree results. That being so, it would appear that her decision to establish a hypothesis was perfectly reasonable, but not all researchers would agree. Moser and Kalton explain the nature of the objections:

> One occasionally hears a survey criticized on the grounds that it did not test a hypothesis or relate to any underlying theory. While there is often substance in this, the criticism is irrelevant to many surveys such as, for instance ... examples of straightforward factual enquiries ... Even these should always be preceded by carefully thought-out decisions about what is, and what is not, worth asking. But only in a trivial sense could it be said that this amounts to a set of hypotheses;

in the narrower sense, implying the testing of a postulated relationship between two or more variables, the formulation of hypotheses is irrelevant to – and impossible for – many fact-collecting enquiries.

(Moser and Kalton 1971: 4)

Punch takes the stronger view that 'there is no point in simply having hypotheses for their own sake'. He considers that

We should by all means formulate hypotheses as predicted answers to research questions, and test them. If not, we can proceed simply with research questions. After all, there is no logical difference between research questions and research hypotheses, when it comes to their implications in design, data collection and data analysis.

(Punch 1998: 40)

We would agree, though views do vary. Some supervisors will invariably require all research students to work to a hypothesis and it would generally be unwise to ignore such advice unless there are very good reasons for doing so. In Helen's case, there was no question of statistical hypothesis testing which would have required not only greater competence in the use of certain descriptive statistical techniques, but also familiarity with appropriate *inferential statistics*. We discuss statistical hypothesis testing and the properties of the null hypothesis later on in Part 3 of this book.

1.3

MOVING ON TO DATA COLLECTION

The first task and the value of pilot studies

Access to admissions records was agreed by the university authorities and all seemed to be well. Helen's first task was to obtain information on students' entry qualifications from university records but in order to ensure that the data collecting would run smoothly she decided to carry out a mini pilot study to include the examination of all the entry qualifications of students as recorded in the university files. The records were made available, and the staff concerned were helpful, but in some cases the records were found to be incomplete or even missing. The fact that the records were unreliable meant that the only way to obtain accurate information about entry qualifications was by asking the students direct. That meant that a far more detailed questionnaire would be required than was originally intended which would involve significantly more work in recording, summarizing and analysing responses. With her supervisor's approval, the original plan to produce a fairly short questionnaire followed by interviews was abandoned and the effectiveness of the survey then depended solely on the quality of the new questionnaire and the comparison of entry qualifications and final degree results.

The one thing we can be sure of in research is that there will be times when things just don't go according to plan. Promised support doesn't always materialize and records are not always in perfect order. No matter how carefully we prepare, there are likely to be hitches and that means that what seems to be ample time in which to do certain jobs is rarely enough. All researchers need to allow more time than seems reasonable – and then a bit more. If no pilot study had been carried out, Helen would have been in real trouble in carrying out her original plans. However, the university records problem was discovered in time. It was a setback but not a total disaster.

The questionnaire

Her second and now much larger task was to design the questionnaire. She had never designed one before and so spent time reading as widely as she could about questionnaire design. Never let anyone tell you it's easy to produce a good questionnaire. It's one of the most taxing techniques facing any researcher. Oppenheim makes the point that 'the world is full of well-meaning people who believe that anyone who can write plain English and has a modicum of common sense can produce a good questionnaire' (Oppenheim 1992: 1). Anyone who believes that is likely to produce a questionnaire containing items which are variously interpreted by respondents and responses which are impossible to analyse. Starting the design process without consulting colleagues and at least some of the guidance provided in the literature on questionnaire design is unwise. As Oppenheim makes clear, books can't provide a template because each questionnaire has to be designed for the specific requirements of the investigation, but there's absolutely no doubt that they go a considerable way to help inexperienced researchers to avoid major pitfalls.

It took numerous drafts of the questionnaire, consultation with colleagues, pilot studies with students on other OT courses, clearance by committees and frequent referring back to the information and guidance in the literature before the final draft was produced. Not all questionnaires take quite so much time. The problem lies more usually with researchers who are too quick off the mark in distributing questionnaires, warts and all, only to discover that it would have been better to have spent more time refining wording and thinking about precisely what information was required. Believe us even the most experienced researchers cannot produce a good one-shot questionnaire. Most will require at least three revisions and often more. That was certainly Helen's experience, but finally, having consulted everybody about everything, having revised and revised again, the questionnaire was deemed to be as good as it could be and it was ready for distribution – until . . .

A hitch

When Helen was ready to distribute the questionnaires, she discovered that a new university procedure for vetting research had been introduced. The new procedure required that copies of the questionnaire plus any supporting documentation should be submitted to the Course Committee for further scrutiny before permission to distribute could be given. This was a perfectly reasonable procedure designed to protect students from being inundated with questionnaires and requests for interviews. Helen's problem was that when she was made aware of this change in the regulations, the Course Committee had just met and was not due to meet for another three months. Goodwill prevailed, steps were taken to obtain approval from individual Course Committee members, but yet again, certain changes were required. Another draft had to be prepared and once again scrutinized before it could be finally approved.

The finally approved questionnaire

The questionnaire was now Helen's only method of data collecting and so it had to include all the items about which she considered information was needed. Twenty-seven individual items covering six pages were required in order to incorporate all the topics, some of which were complicated, particularly those concerned with qualifications, and these caused problems at the analysis stage. However, more of that later. The main items were:

- Background information about students' sex, and age on entry to the course.
- Their entry qualifications (whether studied at school, college or elsewhere).
- Mode of study (full-time, part-time or a combination of both).
- Types of learning environment preferred by respondents (lectures, practical work etc.).
- Anticipated final degree and fieldwork assessment results.
- Plans for further study, if any.
- Plans to practise as an OT (or not).
- Advantages and disadvantages of academic study.
- Academic support provided by people during the course.
- Preferred mode of assessment.

Final degree and fieldwork results were also required, but they had to wait until all results were available in the July before the submission date in the following October – and that put an end to all prospects of holiday before the next term began.

As we have said, and keep on saying, Helen was looking for facts and if, in the case of her student cohort, it was discovered that high entry qualifications did not necessarily correlate with final degree results and fieldwork assessments, then she considered she could take the first step towards discussing the issues of entry qualifications with the university authorities. The mere fact of having gathered together a large amount of information which had only been available formerly in bits and pieces would, she felt, be valuable.

Deciding on what information is needed is one stage in the data-collecting process, but deciding how to obtain that information is quite another. Let's consider the first item on her list which asks respondents to indicate their sex and age on entry to the course. All very straightforward – at least, at first sight. However, before we become too confident, there are a number of issues we need to consider, in particular the limitations of certain question types and of the selected *variables*.

Question types and the selection of variables

In quantitative research, variables need to be measurable (more about measurement later on) and the more precisely defined the variable, the easier it is for the data to be analysed and measured. So, before a final decision can be taken about which variables should be selected for which purpose, there are a few issues to consider. The first relates to question types.

Closed or **structured questions** are those which limit the number and type of possible response. Helen's first question asked respondents to tick a box indicating their gender. **Gender** is a *closed question*. It can have only one of the two values, male or female and because it can only be classified into one of these categories, it is known as a ***dichotomous variable***. Dichotomous variables are easy to manage. They give students no opportunity to add other items or opinions, unless respondents have decided they want nothing to do with your tiresome questionnaire and have decided to play annoying games by ticking both boxes or giving a response like 'Yes'. It has been known.

Does it matter what name is given to variables? Probably not, but it certainly does matter that researchers should understand perfectly well how they will deal with limitations of different types of variable and in any case it's probably as well to get used to using the terminology in common use.

Questions relating to **age** may at first sight seem to be similarly easy to manage but they can present certain difficulties. As always, it's all a question of exactly what information is needed. If Helen had wished to know precisely how old students were when they applied for the OT course, which might have been useful, she would have had to ask the question in a way which gave the necessary information *and*, as always, she would have had to consider what to do with the responses. Let's say there were students who were 18, 19, 20 and up to 50 on the day they first registered for the course. There would be no point in presenting responses in a long list which gave no kind of picture of the age pattern. Some kind of grouping would be needed and perhaps presented in a table or chart. If she had decided she wanted the average age of respondents, she would have had to decide which average (or more accurately measure of central tendency) would be appropriate for her needs and for her sample. Would the *mean*, the *median* or the *mode* provide the most illuminative information? (More about the mean in relation to null hypotheses in Part 3 of the book.) Even before she asked the question, she would have needed to be sure she really wanted that information. Was it necessary for the investigation? Just including questions in case they come in handy is not generally a good idea for any researcher working to a restricted timescale. There's enough to do without clogging up the questionnaire with irrelevancies.

All Helen needed to know was whether respondents were in the 18–20 or 21 and over category. Students who were 21 or over at registration were classified as 'mature' by the university and maturity carried with it certain bursary rights which at the time seemed important. Of course, as Rose and Sullivan remind us,

> one of the problems of transforming any variable like this is a certain loss of information (in this case the age of respondents). In analysis . . . we trade such a loss against the gain we can make for a simplified understanding of the real world.
>
> (Rose and Sullivan 1996: 16)

Perhaps more discriminating information might have emerged by selecting additional groupings to include students who were 30, 40 or 50 and over, even though there were relatively few older students on the course. This was considered, but on balance it seemed that the two categories of 18–20 and 21+ would serve the purpose, and on balance they probably did. So, the first two items on the questionnaire were as follows:

Will you please tick the appropriate box in questions 1 and 2?

(1) SEX   Male ☐   Female ☐

(2) AGE ON ENTRY TO THE
     COURSE   18–20 ☐   21+ ☐

1.4

USING COMPUTER
STATISTICAL PACKAGES

Contrary to popular belief, it's perfectly possible to carry out an analysis of all but very large studies by using nothing more than a pencil and paper. Many people have produced good quality small- to medium-size quantitative research without having the benefit of a computer, but, my goodness, it's tedious. Increasingly these days, quantitative researchers take advantage of appropriate computer programs in order to analyse data and this is what Helen did. Her university provided Statistical Package for the Social Sciences (SPSS) software which she loaded on to her home computer and after a few false starts she found the selected programs fairly easy to use. There are now a good many software packages on the market and your university or organization should be able to offer advice about which type is appropriate for your purpose.

You need to be careful about using statistical packages, however, the main problem being that once you've learnt how, it is really very easy to key in data and even easier for the computer to produce yards and yards of printouts. Yards of printouts can seduce us into believing that they all mean something of importance for our research. That can lead us to include everything which emerges in the vain hope that the examiner will pick out what really is relevant and what isn't. We find it is unwise to irritate examiners and there is nothing more likely to irritate even kind and considerate examiners than to present them with a dissertation which is four times as long as it should be, weighs so much that they are in danger of suffering a double hernia when they pick it up and which is three-quarters full of computer printouts which appear to have little relevance to the topic.

Helen used statistical packages mainly to ease the tedium of manual recording and summarizing, to produce *frequencies* (the number of times each category occurs), *frequency distributions* (how often each category occurs) and well-designed tables and charts. Researchers involved in more complex quantitative studies will require more sophisticated programs but, regardless of the level of complexity, all researchers have to be sure they have selected only those programs which are likely to enable them to *evaluate the importance of the data.*

Preparing data for the computer: *codes* and *coding*

There can be no doubt that computers will do much of the hard work for us – as long as we know how to prepare the data. They have their own rules, the first of which is that if we want them to analyse data, then the data have to be prepared in a form they can accept. Computers work with numbers, not words and that means that variables have to be allocated a number (a code) before they will play our game. Miles and Huberman describe codes as 'tags or labels for assigning units of meaning'. In their view,

> Coding is analysis. To review a set of field notes, transcribed or synthesized, and to dissect them meaningfully, while keeping the relations between the parts intact, is the stuff of analysis. This part of the analysis involves how you differentiate and combine the data you have retrieved and the reflections you make about this information ... Codes are usually attached to 'chunks' of varying sizes – words, phrases, sentences or whole paragraphs, connected or unconnected to a specific setting.
>
> (Miles and Huberman 1994: 56)

They were writing about qualitative research but allocating codes as a first stage in analysis is exactly the same for qualitative or for quantitative investigations. Closed questions are easy to precode because the researcher has already decided which answers are possible and so numeric codes can be allocated before questionnaires are distributed. Open or unstructured questions which ask respondents to give views or opinions are more difficult to precode. Researchers can often make a guess about likely responses, based on experience, hunches, knowledge of the existing research relating to the topic or from pilot studies, but they can't be sure. It might be that their hunches are wide of the mark and so different variables have to be derived from the data. We'll come back to the problems of unstructured and more complex questions later in the book but for the present we'll restrict ourselves to the more straightforward closed questions of gender and age.

In question 1 (gender), code number 1 was allocated to male, 2 for female and 9 for no response. Similarly, in question 2 (age) number 1 was allocated to the 18–20 age category, 2 for the 21 and over group and 9 for no response. Any numbers could have been selected. They are merely labelling devices and are completely arbitrary (see Goulding 1987: 104). Dichotomous variables are at the *nominal scale of measurement* which, as Cohen and Manion point out,

> does no more than identify the categories into which individuals, objects or events may be classified. Those categories have to be mutually exclusive of course, and a nominal scale should also be complete; that is to say it should include all possible classifications of a particular type.
>
> (Cohen and Manion 1994: 128)

Before we continue, it might be helpful to consider the meaning of *'measurement'* in this context. Rose and Sullivan clarify the position as follows:

> Measurement is a way of describing variance. It is *the distribution of objects into two or more classes through the assignment*

of numerals according to rules. Thus, at the most basic level, numeric measurement is simply a form of classification which tells us that one thing is different from another and we make that distinction clear by assigning numerals to each of the different categories of whatever variable we are dealing with.

... Measurement is simply a way of saying that, in respect of some variable, one case is *different* from another. When all that we are talking about is difference, we talk of a nominal measure.

(Rose and Sullivan 1996: 17)

Because these numbers are arbitrary, it's rather important to remember what they represent and that means that a *coding key* is required, regardless of whether recording is to be done manually or by computer. For the first two questions of gender and age, Helen's coding key was:

Table 1 Coding key

CODING KEY	
Gender	1 = male
	2 = female
	9 = no response to this question
Age	1 = 18–20
	2 = 21 and over
	9 = no response to this question

That's all there is to it – *as long as you are working with dichotomous variables.* Helen decided to include the coding on the questionnaire. Obviously more complex questions require more complex coding. There's no single 'right' way to produce a coding/data key. The simpler the better. What is right for you is what works for you. We all have our own quirky ways of doing things, so it's best to try out one or two formats during the pilot studies, select whichever suits you best and stick to it. Helen decided to include the codes on the questionnaire. Some researchers do; others don't. There is no rule that says one way or the other is 'right'.

Manual recorders also need a simple recording and summary sheet, in order to record responses as they come in. Try out different styles and select whichever suits your purposes.

Time to move on now to the third item we have selected from the questionnaire, which relates to students' entry qualifications.

1.5

THE WRETCHED GRIDS

Information about students' entry qualifications was essential because they had to be compared with their final degree results, but Helen had to decide exactly what qualifications information she needed. The answer appears to be 'everything'. She decided to produce detailed grids which asked students to indicate what results they had achieved in a range of subjects, the type of examinations taken, where they studied and whether they studied full- or part-time. Grids are tricky. They ask students to provide answers to two or more questions at the same time, but the more choices that are given, the more complex the analysis becomes.

Let's take a look at the General Certificate of Education at Ordinary Level (GCE O level)/General Certificate of Secondary Education (GCSE) grid.

Four other grids followed, which asked for the same amount of information about a whole range of other qualifications. The questionnaire had been through many drafts and members of vetting committees had occasionally asked for additional items to be included in case they might be useful for some unspecified later purpose. These additions cluttered the questionnaire to such an extent that it became difficult to see what mattered and what didn't. The late changes required by the Course Committee added further complications to the already complex grids and played

Table 2 The qualification grid: GCSE and/or GCE O level

QUALIFICATIONS – GCSE and/or GCE O level

(i) Will you please enter the total **number** of GCSE or
GCE O level (grades A–C) in the box? □

(ii) Please also provide the following information in the grid below.
Whether GCSE or O level; grade obtained; year in which passed
and whether a resit.

Subject	Type	Grade	Year	Resit
e.g. English Language	O	4	1973	✓
English Language				
Maths				
Sociology				
Psychology				
Double Science				
Science				
Biology				
Human Biology				
Physics				
Chemistry				
Others				

(iii) Where did you study for these qualifications?

School □   College □   Other □

(iv) Was this

Full-time □   Part-time □   Full- and part-time □

havoc with the original timescale. The questionnaires had to be distributed before the students were on fieldwork placements and so off campus. Trial analysis had only been done on the early versions and the delays left little time to check whether the original strategies worked for the revised versions. If Helen had tried out her computer programs before distributing the questionnaire, she would have discovered that much of the detail was of no real interest and, moreover, that the computer could not cope with the detail in the grids. She trusted to luck. Unfortunately, luck proved to be an unreliable friend. In fact, no friend at all. In research, it rarely is.

Eventually, she gave up trying to key in the data from what she described as 'the wretched grids', took up a deep breath and set about the task of recording and summarizing manually. She developed a complex system of colour coding, opened file after file which included summaries, categories, duplicate copies and cross-checks. Her study was a mass of box files, envelope files, yellow stick-on reminders of things to do and heaps of paper. Finally, she was able to extract the data manually but it gave her considerable grief and took more time than she could afford. What was even more serious was the fact that the inability to input the data to the computer meant that she was not able to explore relationships between final degree results and, for example, age, sex, entry qualifications and final examination results in the way she had hoped. Even if she had the statistical expertise, which she readily admits she did not, calculating *correlation coefficients* is unwieldy, as will be seen in our discussion of Gilbert Fan's research in Part 2 of the book. Michael Youngman, formerly of the University of Nottingham, provided the following advice to the many student researchers he supervised. It is well worth framing and fixing on study walls in a position where it can't be missed.

At the risk of disillusioning many readers, the first truth of research analysis is that it does not start the day after the last item of data is collected . . . the analytical strategies must be planned early in the research process . . . Deciding upon the actual research procedure will determine the precise nature of the practicable analyses. Selection from within these possible analyses will depend on various considerations such as time available, characteristics of the data, and the outcome of preliminary analyses.

(Youngman 1978: 1)

Absolutely right, and Helen knew this, but the delay caused by the new approval system placed her in a difficult position. All was well in the end, but at a cost. The data were extracted and the findings presented in table and chart form which she was able to produce from the EXCEL software on her computer – and that is generally perfectly satisfactory in descriptive studies. She had been looking for facts and that is what she obtained. She was able to provide a description of students' characteristics, their views about various aspects of the course and the extent to which their entry qualifications related to their final honours degree classification. That was accepted by the examiners as being sufficient for the award of Master of Education. Her research was also valuable because, as she had hoped, she was able to present a picture of the group under investigation to the university authorities which enabled discussions to take place about the possibility of establishing alternative criteria for the admission of students to the OT undergraduate course.

● 1.6

DISCUSSION

As we have indicated earlier, Helen was not in the business of explaining. She had no evidence why some students with lower entry qualifications sometimes did better than others who had higher qualifications though, as she knew the students, she could certainly hazard guesses. All she knew for certain was that many of them did. Description limited the outcomes of the study but no false claims were made, the limitations were fully acknowledged and were accepted by the examiners.

There was never any possibility of generalizing her findings, nor did she ever contemplate generalization because she did not anticipate that her findings were likely to have broader applicability beyond the focus of her study.

Much educational research does seek to generalize and to contribute to the development of educational theory, but it's unlikely that research of the size we are talking about here will achieve such aims. That is certainly not to say that small-scale studies are worthless. Far from it. They may well be relatable to other situations and in other contexts and so, as Bassey (1981: 85) points out, are 'valid forms of educational research'. Helen's research was carried out for a specific purpose and achieved its aims to the extent that it raised the issue of the ever-increasing entry qualifications for the OT degree in her university.

So what, in Helen's opinion, caused difficulties?

We'll start with what, in her view, went sufficiently wrong to take up time she could ill afford and which brought her close to giving up the entire venture.

Problems with the computer

High in her list of bad experiences was trying to get to grips with her new computer, never having used one before. She recalls that

> Sorting out the computer took up an enormous amount of time but I became so desperate that in some ways this experience helped me to learn how to ask for help. At one stage I really reached rock bottom mainly because I felt I ought to be able to cope with things and to sort out my problems. It was a bit humiliating to realize that I couldn't always. I learnt that I didn't need to know everything but I certainly did need to know who to ask for what. And people did help, willingly. There was a lot of personal learning about me by me over that period, but that learning came with scars. Over this learning period, my confidence went up and down, though mostly down. I kept asking myself 'Why am I doing this? Why am I ruining my life? Who am I doing it for?' There were a good many times when I had to keep reminding myself that I've never been a quitter.

'Sorting out the computer' proved to be an ongoing challenge throughout the research. When she reached the stage of presenting data derived from 'the wretched grids' she discovered that the computer had insufficient memory to cope with the required number of tables and charts. She had to open a new file for each table and each graph. Failure to do so resulted in the graphs being replaced by a large red cross in a box! That taught her that it would have been sensible (and obvious with hindsight) to look for advice about the type of computer she needed for her purposes, to take a computer course or at least to have followed the trial-and-error path to computer literacy and to have sorted out all the glitches *before* starting to pay good money in MEd fees to the university. At the start, she really had believed that SPSS would be able to process all the information she keyed in and produce the information in an understandable form. It never occurred to her that responses to the GCSE and other grids would throw up so many variables that everything else associated with the grids ended up a nightmare. She can hardly believe her naivety now but that was the stage when the computer fought back and said 'I'll teach you who's boss.' It was a humiliating experience. She used 'humiliating' rather a lot when she was talking about some of her mistakes. She expected magic, but there's not much magic in research. Magic and luck have to be replaced by a systematic understanding of which approach is appropriate, which computer packages will deliver the goods and what is to be done with the findings. Ah well, it's easy to say but harder to achieve, particularly in the early days of research.

She learnt another hard lesson when she lost half a day's work on the computer because of a power cut. Only then did it occur to her that the computer back-up facility should have been activated and a disk copy made – of everything. Better to copy to excess than to assume everything will be all right. Again, that seems so obvious to her now but then . . . After all, how are you supposed to know these things as a beginner? And it's not only beginners who have lost text because of failing to provide back-up copy. Come on, those of you who are competent computer users, can you honestly say you have never lost any text because you somehow or another managed to forget to save it? Really?

Well, let's leave the computer alone. It's a marvellous tool but not what research is all about. Research is . . . Well, let's leave that alone for a while and mention just one more thing that caused Helen some anxiety at a critical time. That relates to the recording of sources.

Keeping records and recording sources

She was generally careful about recording source material but, at a time when she was writing up her dissertation and was desperately short of time, she could not find the page number for one key quotation. She wasted an entire half day tracking it down and was nearly ready to abandon one whole section when she 'happened across it' on a piece of paper in a box file. Apart from that, she did well with her recording and referencing but omissions like this always seem to happen at critical times.

As all researchers know, no matter whether beginners or experienced, all sources and all details should be recorded. We know of no supervisor who has not emphasized or even reached the stage of nagging student researchers about the importance of keeping complete records of books, journal articles and chapters in books. As they will no doubt have said, 'It's all a question of discipline and managing information effectively' (see Baker 1999: 64–89). However, it's easy to overlook small details which inevitably are the ones you really do need when you come to check references or identify a quotation. And it's not only new researchers who are caught out.

The British Open University employs experienced course team writers and researchers to produce their study guides and readers. They are supported by expert, specialist course team librarians. They have full access to specialist library and on-line resources. Writing is their job, and yet one of these expert, specialist course team librarians writes that

> Unfortunately, from the number of whey-faced academics and researchers about to submit papers or theses who are found panicking in libraries as they desperately search for missing sources, page numbers, authors' initials and so on, it is apparent that even an occasional lapse in recording bibliographic details can result in hours of wasted time at the point when time is particularly short.

Trying to be kind, she continues:

> It is inevitable that you will from time to time lack a similar detail from a reference – sometimes as a result of others'

incorrect referencing – but if you adopt a disciplined approach to information management you will be able to minimize the number of occasions when this occurs.

(Baker 1999: 69)

At the start of research, you never know what might be useful later on so it's always as well to record everything you read – and that does not mean jotting down details on the back of an envelope. That might serve if you have only four or five sources but when you move to 20, 50, 100 or more, the used envelope box is no use. If you are planning to transfer all references to the computer when you get home, it may seem that a used envelope is perfectly satisfactory, but used envelopes have a way of disappearing, particularly if a shopping list happens to be on the other side. If you have a laptop, you might feel confident that you would always have it to hand so a card bibliography is quite unnecessary, but cards weigh nothing and cost very little whereas laptops are heavy and they're expensive. Call us fussy if you like but experience has shown that it's a good idea to have more than one backup source. Even though you'll have everything on your computer, if you have one, you never know. It might break down and swallow your dissertation. You might be burgled. After all, there's a lot of crime about. Of course, you would always have back-up disks, wouldn't you? Of course you would, but a card resource is also nice to have to hand. You know. Just in case.

Decide how and where you are going to record and build up your bibliography. Make sure you *always* note the author's name and initials, date of publication, title (underlined in typescript, inverted commas for articles), place of publication and publisher. It's also a good idea to include the International Standard Book Number (ISBN) because, as all books have their own unique number, it makes it easy for librarians and booksellers to locate them. If your institution does not provide you with their recommended referencing system, ask for it and from then on be consistent. You don't want to waste time starting with one system and then being obliged to change to another.

It's critical to make *an accurate note of all quotations*. Note any omissions by (. . .) and make clear what is a direct quotation and what is your paraphrase. We always think we shall remember matters of detail but we don't and no researchers can run the risk of using other people's words as their own. That is classified as plagiarism and can result in rejection of theses – and worse (see Bell 1999: 48–63).

What did Helen learn from her experience?

She learnt a great deal about literature searching and produced a very good review of the literature. That taught her the importance of reading widely before plunging into data collection. She found the writing difficult but considered the academic discipline helped her to identify key issues, to keep to the point and ruthlessly to eliminate extraneous matter. She also learnt that

- There's no point in trying to design a questionnaire until you know exactly what it is you need to find out – and that means not allowing other people's enthusiasms to encourage you to include items which are irrelevant to the study.
- Possible analytical techniques have to be considered and tried out before decisions can be made about question types or question wording and before data-collecting instruments are designed.
- Statistical packages also have to be tried out before questionnaires are finally designed and distributed – and that includes making sure that the coding systems work.
- Piloting data collecting instruments is essential, not optional.
- Everything takes longer than you think it will and so more time than seems reasonable has to be added to each stage of the research.

All that sounds obvious now but, at the time, it didn't. And yes, she knew she could have obtained a lot more from her data than she did, if only . . . Hindsight is wonderful but often we just have to learn from experience. She was able to extract most of the information she needed from the data even though she gave herself a great deal of work by having to record, summarize and analyse manually. Once she found out how to use the appropriate computer software, she was able to present her findings in graphs, charts, tables and figures and was pleased with the result. Although it was hard to take at the time, she came to accept that there is value in the learning process even when things don't go according to plan and, perhaps more important than anything, she learnt how to ask for help.

FURTHER READING

Bassey, Michael (1981) 'Pedagogic research: on the relative merits of the search for generalization and study of single events', *Oxford Review of Education*, Vol. 7, No. 1, pp. 73–88). Reproduced in Chapter 7 (omitting his appendix on pp. 88–94) in J. Bell, T. Bush, A. Fox, et al. Conducting Small-scale Investigations in Educational Management. London: Harper and Row, in association with the Open University.
This is an excellent article which is worth taking the trouble to locate. Writing about case study, Bassey makes the point that, in many cases, 'the relatability is more important than its generalizability', and provides guidance to investigators on the dangers of generalization on insufficient evidence.

Bell, Judith (1999) *Doing Your Research Project: A Guide for First-time Researchers in Education and Social Science,* 3rd edn. Buckingham: Open University Press.
Chapters 2, 4 and 8 deal with planning the project, keeping records and notes, locating libraries and designing and administering questionnaires.

Denscombe, M. (1998) *The Good Research Guide for Small-scale Social Science Projects.* Buckingham: Open University Press.
Chapters 1 and 6 provide good, clear sections on surveys and questionnaires. Useful checklists are provided at the end of each chapter.

Dixon B.R., Bouma, G.D. and Atkinson, G.B.J. (1987) *A Handbook of Social Science Research: A Comprehensive and Practical Guide for Students.* Oxford: Oxford University Press.

Chapter 4 discusses the selection of variables and the operalization of *concepts*. Good examples are given.

Moser, C.A. and Kalton, G. (1972) *Survey Methods in Social Investigation,* 2nd edn. London: Heinemann.

Chapter 1 (pp. 1–4) gives quality guidance about the nature and purposes of social surveys.

Oppenheim, A.N. (1992) *Questionnaire Design, Interviewing and Attitude Measurement.* London: Pinter.

This new edition of an earlier version is packed with sound advice about pretty well everything on all aspects of questionnaire design and analysis.

Punch, K.F. (1998) *Introduction to Social Research: Quantitative and Qualitative Approaches.* London: Sage.

This is a really good read which covers a whole range of topics relating to 'Research design' (Chapter 5), 'Analysis of quantitative and qualitative data' (Chapters 7 and 10), 'Mixed methods' (Chapter 11) and 'Research writing' (Chapter 12). We particularly like his discussion of 'Research questions' in Chapter 3.

Rose, D. and Sullivan, O. (1996) *Introducing Data Analysis for Social Scientists,* 2nd edn. Buckingham: Open University Press.

Chapter 3 gives ideas about preparing the data and Part III (pp. 81–159) discusses descriptive data analysis in social research. Pages 81–108 deal with frequency distributions, measures of central tendency and measures of dispersion – among other things.

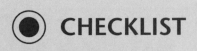 CHECKLIST

1 REMEMBER, all research requires careful planning and that includes ensuring that you have been given formal permission to carry out the research and to be given access to materials and people.	Regardless of whether the research is qualitative or quantitative.
2 Take care to select a topic which is likely to be worth investigating.	It has to sustain your interest throughout the whole period of the research.
3 No methods of data collection can be considered until the purpose of the research is clear.	The *what* question (what exactly do I want to find out?) and the *why* question (why do I want to find it out?) must be settled before the *how* question (how can I obtain these data?) can be considered.
4 A hypothesis is not always necessary in small-scale descriptive studies.	Objectives and/or research questions will serve the purpose well enough.
5 Give careful thought to the selection of question types and the analytical implications of variables.	The more precisely defined the variable, the easier it is for data to be coded and measured.
6 A variable such as gender, which limits the response to only one of two (male or female) is known as a dichotomous variable.	Because responses are known to be only one of two, it is possible to precode them before the data are collected.

7 In quantitative research, all variables need to be measurable.	Measurement is a way of describing variance. It is a way of saying that, in respect of some variable, one case is different from another – not bigger or smaller, better or worse, but only different (Rose and Sullivan 1996: 17).
8 If you are recording and analysing data on a computer, responses have to be coded and a coding key prepared at the time the codes are allocated.	Codes (numbers) are arbitrary and have no numerical significance. They are merely labelling devices.
9 At each stage of the research and before collecting data, CHECK and keep on checking that the wording of items and the selection of variables are appropriate for the task.	Keep going back to the *what, why* and only then to the *how* questions, just to be sure. And never lose sight of the purpose of the research. It's easy to wander.
10 ALWAYS carry out pilot studies. They are a requirement, not an option.	NEVER trust to luck and distribute questionnaires or conduct interviews before you have decided on analytical strategies.
11 REMEMBER always to note all details of sources, including name(s) of author(s), date of publication, title, place of publication and publisher.	And ALWAYS make it clear in your notes which are your words and which are quotations from the book or article. Using other people's words or even very close summaries without acknowledgement will get you into trouble.
12 Make no claims which cannot be substantiated by your data.	In small-scale descriptive studies, it's perfectly reasonable to provide a picture of the group under consideration.

● Part 2

THE EVALUATION STUDY

General area of the research ● ethics committees and codes ● reviewing the literature ● theory, theory building and conceptual frameworks ● flow charts as ways of clarifying thoughts ● question development ● boundaries, concepts to indicators ● operationalization of concepts ● guiding questions ● the questionnaire ● Likert scales ● ordinal data ● pilot studies ● anonymity and confidentiality ● the findings ● the correlation coefficients ● correlation and causation ● making assumptions ● emerging from the bad days.

2.1

BACKGROUND TO THE STUDY, OBTAINING PERMISSION and REVIEWING THE LITERATURE

Introduction

The second study to be considered here is a Master of Education (MEd) dissertation, produced by Gilbert Fan who at the time was a lecturer in the School of Health Sciences at a polytechnic in Singapore (Fan 1998). At one time, Singaporean nursing students worked towards a Certificate in Nursing, but a Diploma in Nursing programme was later introduced in order to prepare nurses for increasingly demanding work commitments. During the course of his work, Gilbert identified what he saw as various worldwide problems in nursing education, not least the decline in student enrolment in nursing programmes; the low status of nursing, which was believed to have contributed to poor recruitment; high attrition rates and the resultant shortage of nurses. He decided to select as his dissertation topic a study of students' perceptions of their diploma programme and of the nursing profession in general. He knew this study would be of interest to him personally but he anticipated it would also add to the School of Health Sciences' understanding of the diploma programme from the perspective of the first cohort of students to graduate. However, he was aware of the fact that the survey might raise some sensitive issues and, that being so, he had to make absolutely sure that he had full, formal approval to carry out the research before he even began to work through the first stages of planning.

Obtaining permission

As we all know, permission always has to be obtained before any research can be carried out. It should never be assumed that it's 'bound to be all right' – and that applies whether we are researching in our own organization or somewhere else. However, health and social care providers have particularly stringent requirements designed to ensure participants are not in any way put at risk, are fully aware of the purpose of the research and know their rights. Hospitals and many university departments involved in research with human subjects will have *ethics committees* which have responsibility for ensuring that any research proposals conform to approved principles, and this is good practice – in the interests not only of those being researched, but also of those doing the researching. (see Cohen and Manion 1994: 381; Hart and Bond 1995: 198–201; Blaxter *et al.* 1996: 145–9 and Bell 1999: 38–43.)

In Gilbert's case due care was taken to conform to all polytechnic, hospital and other professional requirements. His study was approved in principle by the director of the School of Health Sciences and it was agreed that all 234 registered final year Diploma in Nursing students of the first diploma cohort could be included in the investigation

The review of the literature

The first stage was to carry out what proved to be an extensive literature review into the current body of published research findings which included reports of research into student selection and admission criteria; curricula; types of nursing education and nursing competences; teaching and clinical supervision in nursing education programmes; the relationship between nursing education and the profession; and nursing as a career choice. This not only allowed Gilbert to be aware of developments in nursing education in many parts of the world, but it also enabled him to consider ways in which other researchers had structured their research, some of which gave him ideas about possible structures for his own investigation.

The published literature, which Wolcott (1992) described as 'theory first', provided the theoretical base for his study. Jan Gray, whose investigation into truancy is considered in Part 4 of the book, aimed to generate theory from her findings 'theory after', but she still carried out an extensive review of the literature, as do most researchers. Hers was a three-year, full-time PhD study, though even this timescale was tight for theory generation. Gilbert, and all other part-time MEd researchers, are limited to a year or less for their dissertation and for them a theory generation study would have been out of the question.

Theory and conceptual frameworks

Before we move on to the planning stage of his study, it might be as well to spend a little more time considering the terms *'theory'* and *'conceptual framework'* used in the literature. Miles and Huberman's definition of theory building and of conceptual frameworks seem to us to express very clearly the process Gilbert carried out in the move from concepts to variables. They write that

> Theory building relies on a few general constructs that subsume a mountain of particulars. Terms such as 'stress' or 'role conflict' are typically labels we put on bins containing a lot of discrete events and behaviors. When we assign a label to a bin, we may or may not know how all the contents of the bin fit together, or how this bin relates to another. But any researcher, no matter how inductive in approach, knows which bins to start with and what their general contents are likely to be. Bins come from theory and experience and (often) from the general objectives of the study envisioned. Laying out those bins, giving each a descriptive or inferential name, and getting some clarity about their interrelationships is what a conceptual framework is all about.
>
> (Miles and Huberman 1994: 18)

2.2

THE PREPARATION

Gilbert's preparation was extremely thorough and during the initial planning stages he frequently used flow-charts to explore general ideas. He found them helpful, as have the other researchers, in order to keep his thoughts in line with his topic, to clarify some of the more complex concepts and to assist in the establishment of a conceptual framework. Figure 1 provides an example of how he decided on the core issue and then began to put his 'bins' into place around the core.

He took time over the planning and identification of issues, consulted colleagues and students, took account of their comments and then produced four first-thoughts questions which were:

1 What are the general perceptions among nursing students of their Diploma in Nursing programme?
2 How satisfied are the students with their Diploma in Nursing programme?
3 What are the students' general perceptions of the nursing profession?
4 What is the likelihood of students pursuing a career in nursing on graduation?

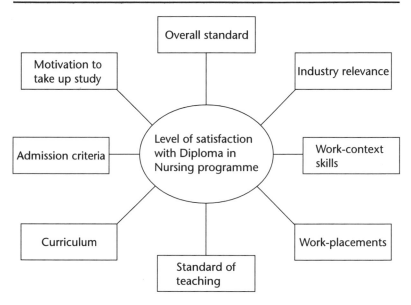

Figure 1   Factors influencing students' level of satisfaction with the Diploma in Nursing programme

These questions covered the general areas to be investigated, but they were not yet sufficiently specific to be answerable. More work was needed on question development.

The question development stage is quite often hurried but it's unwise to move too quickly on to specific research questions because, as Punch warns:

Sometimes the more abstract concepts of the research area . . . are not enough to get the process of identifying and developing research questions started. When that happens, it is good to focus on . . . 'What are we trying to find out?' The focus on this question almost always shows that there is 'much more here than meets the eye'. The topic expands, and many questions are generated. What perhaps seemed simple and straightforward becomes complicated, many-sided and full of possibilities . . . [The question generating stage] is a mixture of question subdivision, where we split a general question into its component parts, and of disentangling the different questions from each other . . . it is ordering these questions, and progressively developing focus.

(Punch 1998: 36)

It is also about drawing boundaries. Question development has to take place but there must be a limit to the number of possibilities that can be considered. It's perhaps worth mentioning at this stage that we are still at the 'What are we trying to find out?' stage. No thought can yet be given to method. It is pre-empirical and decisions about 'How are we going to find this out?' come later.

Gilbert still had some way to go before he could move to the stage of planning specific research questions.

Concepts to indicators

In quantitative research, ways have to be found of measuring responses, but terms like 'perception' and 'satisfaction' are concepts and concepts cannot be seen, observed and measured. Rose and Sullivan provide guidance about this particular dilemma of quantitative research as follows:

> By definition, *concepts* are abstractions by which we select and order our impressions of the world. They are mental constructs and are, therefore, not observable . . . If we wish to understand something about class (a concept, and, therefore, part of our theoretical language and not observable) what can we observe . . . which manifests class?
>
> (Rose and Sullivan 1996: 12/13)

They suggest that indicators of 'class' might include occupation and employment status and this would move one step from the concept of 'class' to the measurable variables of occupation and unemployment status. This is the route Gilbert followed. By identifying ways in which concepts such as perception or satisfaction might be observed, he was systematically drawn into the process of producing a route from the concepts of perception and satisfaction to measurable variables.

He tried out various categories and subcategories before he felt sufficiently confident to focus on the following eight areas:

1 admission criteria;
2 curriculum;
3 relevance of the curriculum to the profession;
4 quality of teaching and clinical supervision;
5 work placements;
6 skills acquired;
7 industry sponsorships; and
8 the overall quality of the programme.

All eight were then further focused in the following way in order to continue the process of moving from the general to the specific.

2.3

OPERATIONALIZATION OF THE CONCEPTS

Each of the eight areas had to be transposed into ***measurable indicators***. There was a great deal more to be done before he was finally satisfied, but Table 3 illustrates how he began.

Gilbert now had a framework within which he could identify the different areas about which he needed information. The eight topics had been developed into statements but they needed further development before they were ready to be incorporated into a questionnaire. He decided to produce guiding questions for each of the above eight areas and we've selected the first of the eight categories, **admission criteria**, as an example of the way the questions expanded the topic.

Guiding questions on 'admission criteria'

1 Did the students feel that their secondary education had adequately prepared them for their nursing studies?
2 Of those who replied positively to (1), what was their educational background prior to joining this course of study (that is the Diploma in Nursing)?
3 What were the students' perceptions of existing academic admission criteria?

4 For those who wish the existing academic criteria to be changed, what was their educational background?

5 What were the students' views on the impact of lowering existing academic admission criteria?

6 Of those who were concerned with the lowering of the academic admission criteria, how many of them also value 'interest' and 'pre-selection test' as important prerequisites for nursing studies?

7 Is there any association between students' views on 'interest' and 'pre-selection tests' as important admission criteria and their aspirations to pursue a career in nursing?

Table 3 First steps in operationalizing the concepts

1 The admission criteria	The relevance of students' secondary education in preparing them for the nursing programme. Their opinion about the existing academic and non-academic criteria for admission such as secondary school results, interest and pre-selection test. Their perception of the relationship between admission criteria and demand for the programme.
2 The relevance of students' nursing curriculum	The comprehensiveness of the curriculum; and the balance between theoretical and practical components of the programme.
3 Industry relevance	The relevance of the programme to the needs of the health care industry and the profession.
4 The quality of teaching and clinical supervision	The standard of teaching and the adequacy of clinical supervision.
5 The work placements	The adequacy of work placements, students' learning of and confidence in practical skills for nursing functions.

Table 3   cont'd

6 Skills acquired	Work skills (interpersonal, communication, thinking and problem-solving); nursing functions.
7 Industry sponsorship	Importance and relevance of sponsorship, in particular: reasons for taking or not taking up the sponsorship, and relationship between sponsorship and career in nursing.
8 Overall quality of the programme	Students' attitude towards the programme; level of difficulty of the programme, and overall standard of the programme.

The size of the task

The procedures carried out for 'admission criteria' were replicated for the other seven areas (relevance of students' nursing curriculum; industry relevance; quality of teaching and clinical supervision; work placements; skills acquired; industry sponsorship and overall quality of the programme). Gilbert knew what information he required from students and, at last, he was able to consider how best to obtain the data. The research had moved from 'What do I want to find out?' to 'How can I find this out?'

He was a single researcher working part-time to a limited timescale, which in his case was about one year. His preparation had, as you can imagine, taken a considerable amount of time and it would have been impossible in anything like the timescale for him to carry out the number of interviews which would have been necessary in order to obtain all the data he needed. It had become apparent that a questionnaire was likely to be the most feasible data-collecting instrument. Now, said quickly, that seems to be perfectly reasonable, but consider the number of items associated with the admission criteria category alone. Multiply the number of tasks involved in the other seven categories and that gives you some idea of the work involved.

His supervisor could foresee problems but Gilbert was determined to produce a thorough job. He had permission to survey members of the first cohort of nursing diploma students, with their permission, and he was determined that all 234 should be included. The combination of the number of variables involved and the size of the population meant that he had a major research task on his hands – but nothing was about to make him reduce its size and complexity. His supervisor recalls that he made several attempts to persuade him to be less ambitious, but in the end just had to let him go ahead. After all, it was Gilbert's dissertation, not his supervisor's.

The design and wording of the questionnaire

Gilbert was ready to design his questionnaire. It would have been of little use to ask students 'What are your general perceptions of your diploma in nursing?' If he had, it would have produced responses such as 'Not bad', 'Too hard', 'Didn't like the science' – or no response at all. Questions had to be worded in ways which respondents would understand. Even Gilbert realized that if he designed a questionnaire with many different types of question, he would be giving himself complex and time-consuming problems of analysis. He decided to make use of a Likert scale for most items on the questionnaire, and that required him to translate questions into statements.

Likert scales ask respondents to indicate rank order of agreement or disagreement with a given statement or statements which are generally, though not always, on a three-, five- or seven-point range. Answers are then scored from strongly approve or strongly agree down to strongly disapprove or strongly disagree. They consist of **ordinal data** or *ordinal scales* which arise where items are **rated** or **ranked**. As Cohen and Manion point out, these scales need to be treated with caution because they arrange 'individuals or objects in a series ranging from the highest to the lowest according to the particular characteristic being measured' (Cohen and Manion 1994: 128). So, they do not indicate absolute quantities, nor can we assume that the intervals between the numbers are equal. They distinguish order, but that's all.

So, if we were to rank 10 people in terms of their ability to coordinate a team, we could not assume that the individual who selected the top item (say 'very strongly agree') had 10 times the ability of the lowest.

Gilbert chose a six-point scale, to eliminate the neutral centre point. The example we give below turns guiding question 5 into a statement and when we move on to give other 'admission criteria' Likert statements you will see that they similarly relate to the other guiding questions. Gilbert's scale could have been designed in the following way where students are asked to circle the appropriate number:

If the present educational criteria for the diploma in nursing programme are lowered, more people will be encouraged to take up nursing as a course of study.

Very strongly disagree	Strongly disagree	Disagree	Agree	Strongly agree	Very strongly agree
1	2	3	4	5	6

He preferred the following form where respondents are asked to circle VSD (very strongly disagree), SD (strongly disagree), D (disagree), A (agree), SA (strongly agree) or VSA (very strongly agree).

If the present educational criteria for the diploma in nursing programme are lowered, more people will be encouraged to take up nursing as a course of study.

VSD SD D A SA VSA

There are certain merits in this form, not least the fact that the items take up less space, and that matters in a long questionnaire. He chose to put the 'very strongly disagree' first for most items, but he could equally have started with 'very strongly agree'. It was immaterial which way round the item was presented, as long as he remembered which number applied to which category.

THE QUESTIONNAIRE

Inevitably, we don't have the space to include the entire questionnaire here, but as an example of the format, let's look now at the questionnaire items which relate to the guiding questions on **admission criteria**, namely items 4, 5(a), (b) and (c), 6, 7, 8 and 9.

The pilot exercise

All ready now for the distribution of the questionnaire? Not quite. All research instruments need to be piloted, no matter how small the investigation. We may think our questionnaires, interview or observation schedules are just perfect but our respondents might have other ideas. What is perfectly clear to us may not convey the meaning intended to others. Gilbert piloted his questionnaire by distributing 40 drafts to students, senior nursing colleagues and non-nursing colleagues. He found their comments helpful. They pointed out that the meaning of some questions was not clear. Some spotted redundancy in one or two questions and one was asking for two things. He took note of what was said, adjusted wording and format where necessary and eliminated a few items altogether. The original 87 items were finally reduced to 76 – still a sizeable number, but the pilot respondents had little difficulty

Table 4 Questionnaire items on admission criteria

4 My secondary education prepared me
adequately for my nursing studies.   VSD SD D A SA VSA

5 The present educational criteria for
admission to the Diploma in Nursing
programmes should
  (a) be lowered.   VSD SD D A SA VSA
  (b) have its GCE O level credit points
    raised.   VSD SD D A SA VSA
  (c) be raised to GCE A level standard.   VSD SD D A SA VSA

6 If the present educational criteria for entry
to the Diploma in Nursing programme are
lowered more people will be encouraged
to take up nursing as a course of study.   VSD SD D A SA VSA

7 If the present educational criteria for entry
to the Diploma in Nursing programme are
lowered the status of nursing will fall.   VSD SD D A SA VSA

8 'Interest' in nursing as an entry criterion
is more educationally important than
qualifications.   VSD SD D A SA VSA

9 Pre-selection tests should be administered
to select the right candidate for the
Diploma in Nursing programme.   VSD SD D A SA VSA

Note: GCE O level examinations are still held in Singapore, even though GCSE has
taken their place elsewhere.

in completing the questionnaire in reasonable time and all seemed
to be well. He was fairly satisfied with the design and wording of
the questionnaire, gave some thought to how he would analyse
his data and took advice about which computer statistical packages would be best for his purposes, but he trusted to luck and
did not carry out trial analyses. He was luckier than Helen had
been and his planned analytical strategy worked well.

Grouping responses

In quantitative research, we are always looking for patterns, similarities and items of particular significance. It's never enough to present raw data as if that were the end of the matter, and just listing students' responses to the 76 items would not only have been tedious but would have meant little to Gilbert or to his readers. Decisions had to be made about how the data would be analysed, and that meant deciding on appropriate groupings.

Look at the following four categories – admission criteria; curriculum; industry relevance and the quality of teaching and clinical supervision. Then look at the way *Likert* statements were grouped under those headings.

As you see, 'admission criteria' items followed the 4–9 sequence, but others were not necessarily sequential. For example, 'curriculum' occurred in items 15, 18, 22 and 52; 'industry relevance' in items 16, 39, 41 and 46 and 'quality of teaching and clinical supervision' in items 19 and 20(c). The order of items is immaterial, but before questionnaires were distributed, Gilbert had worked out which item would fit into which group.

The distribution of the questionnaire

Questionnaires and an accompanying letter were distributed to final year nursing students of the Diploma in Nursing programme during the first two weeks of their second semester. Permission was obtained from the Director of the School of Health Sciences to administer the questionnaires during the first sociology tutorial of the semester. They were administered in twelve batches over two weeks, with the assistance of one of Gilbert's colleagues, and most students took about twenty minutes to complete. It was made clear that participation was voluntary, though the fact that students were invited to complete the questionnaire in tutorial time would undoubtedly have contributed to the high level of participation. In fact, 97.4 per cent of the 234 students returned completed questionnaires.

The letter served several purposes. It explained the purpose of

Table 5 Grouping of questionnaire items

Variables	Question number	Items	Responses
Admission criteria	4	My secondary education prepared me adequately for my nursing studies.	VSD SD D A SA VSA
	5(a)	The present educational criteria for admission to the Diploma in Nursing programme should be lowered.	VSD SD D A SA VSA
	5(b)	The present educational criteria for admission to the Diploma in Nursing programme should have its GCE O level credit points raised.	VSD SD D A SA VSA
	5(c)	The present educational criteria for admission to the Diploma in Nursing programme should be raised to GCE A level standard.	VSD SD D A SA VSA
	6	If the present educational criteria for entry to the Diploma in Nursing programme are lowered more people will be encouraged to take up nursing as a course of study.	VSD SD D A SA VSA
	7	If the present educational criteria for entry to the Diploma in Nursing programme are lowered the status of nursing will fall.	VSD SD D A SA VSA
	8	'Interest' in nursing as an entry criterion is more important than educational qualifications.	VSD SD D A SA VSA
	9	Pre-selection tests should be administered to select the right candidate for the Diploma in Nursing programme.	VSD SD D A SA VSA

Category	Item	Statement	Response
Curriculum	15	The present nursing curriculum is broad enough to cover almost every basic aspect of nursing as required by hospitals.	VSD SD D A SA VSA
	18	The theoretical component of the Diploma in Nursing programme is too highly emphasized.	VSD SD D A SA VSA
	22	A nurse does not need a strong theoretical base in nursing to practise nursing.	VSD SD D A SA VSA
	52	What other subjects would you like to include in your present curriculum?	Open-ended question. Answers need to be categorized.
Industry relevance	16	The present nursing curriculum meets the needs of hospitals.	VSD SD D A SA VSA
	39	The nursing curriculum should be determined by the needs of the profession.	VSD SD D A SA VSA
	41	I feel that I am not adequately trained for a full-time nursing job.	VSD SD D A SA VSA
	46	The Diploma in Nursing programme seems likely to meet the needs of employers.	VSD SD D A SA VSA
Quality of teaching and clinical supervision	19	I find the overall standard of teaching in the Diploma in Nursing programme to be good.	VSD SD D A SA VSA
	20(c)	In terms of my work placements, I feel that there is not enough supervision given.	VSD SD D A SA VSA

the research, informed students that participation was voluntary, gave instructions about how the items were to be completed and guaranteed that no individual would be identified in the final report. They were invited to provide information about their age (on a specified date), gender, highest educational level attained, secondary school stream (Science/Technical/Arts/Commerce or Other) and their language stream (English or non-English). Obtaining basic background information of this kind is often useful to enable researchers to provide a thumbnail sketch of the population as a starting point in the study.

The vexed question of anonymity and confidentiality

Before we move on to the findings of the research, a warning about promises of anonymity and/or confidentiality. Gilbert could legitimately make such promises because the structure of his questionnaire made it impossible for him or anyone else to identify individuals and also, as the questionnaires were distributed in the sociology seminar, there was no need to follow up non-respondents. If any completed questionnaires were not returned, that was because the students declined to complete them. However, we are aware of the fact that some researchers can be rather imprecise about their use of these terms – and that their understanding has on occasion differed from the understanding of their respondents.

Sapsford and Abbott, writing about interviews, remind us that

A first principle of research ethics – to be found in all the various codes of conduct imposed by professional and academic organizations – is that the subjects of the research should not be *harmed* by it. You might think this fairly obvious, but some quite startling breaches of it have been committed in the course of research. . . . It is for this reason, among others, that we generally promise informants confidentiality or anonymity in surveys or 'unstructured' interviewing projects; interviewing is intrusive, but having your personal details splashed in identifiable form across a research project is even more intrusive.

(Sapsford and Abbott 1996: 318–19)

In their view,

Confidentiality is a promise that you will not be identified or presented in identifiable form, while *anonymity* is a promise that even the researcher will not be able to tell which responses came from which respondent.

(p. 319)

These definitions are sound and the implications of each need to be clearly understood before any such promises are made.

Gilbert made no promises he could not honour. He had thoroughly prepared the research and had obtained official permission to carry it out in his polytechnic. He had piloted, revised and restructured his questionnaire until he was as satisfied as he could be that he had a workable instrument. Questionnaires had been distributed and returned. Crunch time had arrived. He had reached the stage of examining returns, recording, summarizing and analysing the data, presenting them in a form which was acceptable (and understandable) to his supervisor, his examiners, his readers and to himself.

We should perhaps mention that when he began his research, he had little knowledge of statistical computer packages and it would probably have been possible for him to ask a friend or a colleague at work to carry out the analysis for him. However, he decided to do the job himself. He asked for help, consulted his supervisor and a locally based friend who was experienced in computer analysis and decided that a standard statistical package would serve his purposes. He then set about the task of learning how to use it. Though this took time, it proved to be worth the effort because the experience helped him to know what the analysis was saying and to understand and evaluate the significance of his data.

2.5

THE FINDINGS

The *descriptive statistics*

228 (97.4 per cent) of the students returned questionnaires, 82 of whom (36 per cent) had one or more missing response. One

Table 6   Age of final-year nursing students

Age	Number of students	Percentage of students	19–21 group total
19	50	22.0	
20	73	32.2	178 (78.4%)
21	55	24.2	
			22–24 group total
22	26	11.5	
23	11	4.8	42 (18.5%)
24	5	2.2	
			25–27 group total
25	4	1.8	
26	2	0.9	7 (3.1%)
27	1	0.4	

return had 15 missing responses and so was excluded from the study. Let's look at a few of the findings, starting with the **age** of final year nursing students. What does this tell us? Well, it tells us that 78.4 per cent of students were in the 19–21 age group in the third year of the diploma programme, which is probably to be expected; that 21.6 per cent were in the 22–27 age group, with a sharp tailing off as the age increased. However, the question that needs to be asked before presenting any findings is 'What purpose does this information serve?' and 'Is this the best way to present the findings?' In this case, given that the majority of students start their diploma studies straight from school at around the ages of 16 or 17, the fact that almost four-fifths of them were in the 19–21 age range in their final year of the three-year diploma course provides no surprises. However, as the number of students in the 25–27 range is very small, perhaps it might have been clearer to indicate the age groups on the following lines:

Table 7   Grouped age of final-year nursing students

Age range	Group total	Cumulative percentage
19–21	178	78.4
22–24	42	96.9
25–27	7	100

You have to decide which you consider best suits these particular data. There's no point in providing both, so which is it to be? If neither table suits, what other format would be better and would additional commentary highlight any issues of particular note? One of the great advantages of using computer packages is that they allow us to produce graphs and tables fairly easily, once we know how, as long as we give the right instructions. That means we can produce alternatives and then see which illustrate the data best. Of course, having done all the work of reviewing the alternatives, the temptation to include them all can be compelling, but RESIST. Select only the most appropriate. The examiners will be in the picture after studying the first.

Perhaps the second might illustrate another aspect of the data, but the tenth? Take care. Irritable people, examiners.

Let's see what Gilbert found about **gender** and **educational level**.

Table 8 Gender and qualifications on entry to the course

Background characteristics		Count	Percentage
Gender	Male	23	10.1
	Female	204	89.9
	Total	227	100.0
Educational level			
	O level	199	89.6
	A level	23	10.4
	Total	222	100.0

It's perhaps not surprising that nearly 90 per cent of the students were female because nursing has long been a mainly female occupation but Gilbert also asked for educational qualifications. Anything interesting here? Well, as most students start the diploma course straight from school, it's to be expected that most of them had only O level entry qualifications, so not too much of interest. Anything else?

Look at these results again. Is it merely a coincidence that there are 23 men in the sample and 23 of the total sample were A level entrants to the diploma course? Might this mean that only the men were A level entrants? If that were true, then would that be interesting? Well, it might but it's dangerous to make assumptions. When Gilbert took a more detailed look at his data, he discovered that only one man had A levels on entry to the programme. *Coincidences can lead us to assume associations which may not be there*, so take care.

* * *

There's nothing wrong in merely presenting *frequency distributions* (the number of occurrences in each category) and percentage distributions (the percentage of cases in each category) if facts are all that are required, but Gilbert decided he needed to know more about possible association between areas such as students' decisions to pursue a career in nursing and their experiences of nursing education.

Look at the following table. What, if anything, does it tell you?

Table 9 The influence of nursing education on students' decisions to pursue a career in nursing

| | | I am likely to take up a career in nursing | | |
		Agree	Disagree	Total
Even though I am almost into my final year of nursing studies,	Agree	14 (25.5%)	41 (74.5%)	55 (100.0%)
I never intended to	Disagree	137 (80.1%)	34 (19.9%)	171 (100.0%)
become a nurse.	Total	151 (66.8%)	75 (33.2%)	226 (100.0%)
Since starting my diploma in nursing programme, I have	Agree	131 (81.9%)	29 (18.1%)	160 (100.0%)
increased my interest	Disagree	20 (29.9%)	47 (70.1%)	67 (100.0%)
in becoming a nurse.	Total	151 (66.5%)	76 (33.5%)	227 (100.0%)
Since starting my diploma in nursing	Agree	9 (18.0%)	41 (82.0%)	50 (100.0%)
studies, I no longer	Disagree	141 (88.1%)	35 (19.9%)	176 (100.0%)
aspire to become a nurse.	Total	150 (66.4%)	76 (33.6%)	226 (100.0%)

Note: Correlations (in the order of presentation above) with 'career in nursing': Kendall's tau_b: .534; .517; .549.

At first glance all the percentages and totals in this table might just look like description in that all they do is summarize responses. However, look again. They go further than this because Gilbert has put the results of each item into two groups: those students who agreed and those who disagreed (remember he used a 6-point Likert scale). He has then ***cross-tabulated*** these results with the three items which ask students for their view of nursing now they have almost completed their diploma, against their likelihood of taking up nursing as a career.

Cross-tabulation is a descriptive statistic. It merely shows numbers giving one answer (or a grouped answer as in this case) for one item against those for another. You might have expected that if students began the diploma course wanting to be nurses, their diploma experience would not have altered this position, and this seems to be the case. But the cross-tabulations give no idea of the strength of the association, or relationship. To discover this Gilbert had to calculate the appropriate *correlation coefficients*.

The correlation coefficients

Look again at Table 9 and at the note at the bottom of the table which states:

> Correlations (in the order of presentation above) with 'career in nursing': Kendall's tau_b: .534: .517: .549.

This requires a little explanation. For a start, it tells us that the statistical test used was Kendall's tau_b which is the name of the measure of association between variables of ordinal (rank) order. Gilbert is correlating 'I am likely to take up a career in nursing' (the constant) with:

1 Even though I am almost into my final year of nursing studies, I never intended to become a nurse.
2 Since starting my diploma in nursing programme, I have increased my interest in becoming a nurse.
3 Since starting my diploma in nursing studies, I no longer aspire to become a nurse.

The correlation coefficients produced with 'career in nursing' were: (1) 0.534; (2) 0.517 and (3) 0.549.

It would have been difficult, time-consuming, and easy to make mistakes if Gilbert had attempted to calculate these correlation coefficients manually, but the appropriate computer program made the process relatively painless. In his case, the important point was not so much that he should be able to demonstrate that he could carry out the calculations manually but that he knew what information he wished to obtain from his data, which statistical test would be appropriate and what the results indicated. So what did they indicate?

The correlation coefficients provided evidence of a modest association between the constant (I am likely to take up a career in nursing) and each of the three statements in the left-hand column of the table. 'Association' is the key word. Gilbert makes no claim that students' nursing education *caused* their decision to pursue a career in nursing. To have made stronger claims would have involved a much more complex study testing multi-causal factors well beyond the scope of a Masters dissertation.

Correlation and *causation*

All correlation coefficients must be treated with similar caution. Even if two variables have a *high* positive correlation this does not necessarily mean that one is the cause of the other. McMillan and Schumacher (1984: 195) provide a very neat example of this where they show that there is a high positive correlation between the body weight of pupils of ages 5–12 and their reading achievement. There is no doubting the correlation and it might suggest (if you believed correlation = causation) that fattening pupils up could increase their reading achievements! Of course there is a third variable, not mentioned so far, namely 'age'. Age also has a high positive correlation with reading achievement and, we think you'll agree, is likely to have a stronger causal link than weight.

* * *

There are many types of research which do not require statistical or computational expertise, but in much quantitative research there will inevitably be requirements for statistical analysis. That does not mean that all quantitative researchers have to be skilled statisticians. Gilbert always claimed to be 'scared of stats' but he asked for advice, found out what certain statistical applications would do and then learnt how to understand, use and make the most of what the selected programs offered.

2.6

DISCUSSION

As is the case in all the dissertations and theses considered in this book, we have only been able to draw on a very small part of Gilbert's overall research and we have concentrated on the quality of his planning and preparation, which we consider to be very sound. If these stages are hurried and the selection of methods made too soon, the conclusions are likely to be questionable. He worked within the limits of his time, expertise and environment though, like many another researcher, was disappointed not to be able to do all he would have hoped. His conclusions and recommendations remain confidential to his polytechnic but even though they remain unpublished, they made a valuable contribution to the polytechnic's information base. At a personal level, the process of completing the dissertation enabled him to learn a great deal about doing research and about his researched topic. However, not everything had gone entirely according to plan. It would perhaps have been remarkable if it had. Like many other part-time adult students, he had other commitments, not least the demands of a full-time job.

He was studying at a distance (a very great distance in fact) which sometimes caused communication problems and he experienced some difficulty in gaining access to relevant literature, particularly journal articles. Generally, academic library provision in Singapore is good, but before the establishment of the Diploma in Nursing, nursing programmes had been at certificate level, which only demanded O level entry qualifications. As a result, there was a shortage of quality nursing literature at the time he was carrying out his investigation. Never one to admit defeat, he looked for materials outside Singapore. He writes:

> I went twice to Australia, mainly for holidays, but beforehand, I identified which universities had good health science programmes and each visit I spent about two days visiting libraries. I consulted their stock of education research books and photocopied relevant nursing articles in the journals. I got over a hundred articles. They provided me with good source material, but the shortage of materials in Singapore meant that my literature review drew mainly on research done in the UK, America and Australia.

Not everyone has the will, the means or the opportunity to go to such lengths, but Gilbert was nothing if not determined. He found the literature search part of his study to be particularly valuable:

> The literature research helped me a great deal. The reading gave me some direction and focus. I was able to discover how other countries, colleges and articles plan their nursing curriculum and the articles more or less confirmed most of my thoughts about nursing curricula. I got more confident as I read more articles because I found that we were all talking about the same thing and that made me comfortable that I was on the right track.

Many very experienced adult students have commented about the loss of confidence at some stage in their research and anxiety about whether or not they were on the right track. Gilbert had never done a major research study and, like many others, he experienced periods of frustration:

> I was very nervous in the initial period because I had never done anything like this before. I didn't know what to expect

and there were so many things I didn't know how to do. I found it difficult to decipher what was important and what wasn't. I got disappointed and got into a sort of 'giving up syndrome'. Once I got past the 'giving up' stage, it was like sunshine days all the time – though with a few mood swings when I just couldn't get the data and couldn't seem to achieve what I wanted. I think it's very important for people to know that when they get stuck into the giving up syndrome, they'd better not get drowned by their own expectations and disappointments. There's always a way out and luckily I found the way out. Otherwise I might well have given up.

On some occasions, when work commitments were heavy, he had to put the research on hold. He didn't give up but when he resumed his research planning, he had to keep going back to remind himself where he was and what he had done before. It's always a bad time when that happens because it seems such a waste of time, but sometimes research just has to be put to one side until some pressure period is dealt with. Gilbert was helped by the fact that he was really interested in his topic and in reading the literature. He was similarly interested in sorting out the methodology and analysing the data. He looked forward to seeing the outcomes and reporting on findings and so he emerged successfully from the bad days.

He had good support from his polytechnic, which was essential in view of the fact that he was actually planning to carry out an evaluation of the diploma programme and for that he needed the support and encouragement of colleagues. He also had good help from his dissertation supervisor and from a locally based friend who was an experienced researcher. It all helped. He was in touch with his supervisor regularly by e-mail and generally received prompt replies to his queries, though if there were delays he always felt very anxious about whether he was on the right track or not.

He was asked whether eventually things had gone according to plan.

Initially, I thought I wanted to do a descriptive, qualitative kind of thing because I am very afraid of stats. In the end, it came out more stats than qualitative because after a lot of trials, the questions asked were not much of a qualitative nature. Most of them had to be measured or grouped into domains, so I found it was natural to move into a statistical kind of survey. There were not many open ended questions but I grouped the responses and named them – and after that I measured them and so it became quantitative again.

Gilbert may have been 'afraid of stats' but in fact by the time he finished his dissertation, he had a very adequate statistical base. Moreover, he was computer competent, had taken an SPSS course, gained experience in the use of statistical packages and knew when and where to ask for help if he ran into difficulties. As a result, he had a head start over Helen who had to spend a lengthy period coping with the foibles of her new computer before she could begin her research.

Keying the data into the computer program was a massive job which took a great deal of time. At that stage, he became demoralized. In an interview with his supervisor, he said:

You told me I was too ambitious. It was still very painful to me to realize that but subsequently everything worked well. The greatest challenge and the greatest excitement was when I started to analyse the data. When I started the cross-tabulations and when I saw the interesting results, that kept me going. I really enjoyed doing all the analysis. It was interesting to me because I was involved in the teaching and it was great to see how students look at things. I saw the raw data and then had to do a statistical interpretation of the data. The results kept me alight.

All's well that ended well?

Oh yes. Very well, though it was not possible for Gilbert to do some of the analysis he had hoped for. He realized, after the event, that he needed more detailed information about the students' educational background. Remember that this research was carried out in Singapore where GCE O levels are still provided and all the scores of the best five O levels are added together to produce an aggregate point score. It would have been helpful to know students' aggregate points and then to have carried out an analysis of who performed well, and who did not; who intended to take up a post in nursing after the diploma and who did not; to have discovered whether an initial firm interest in nursing and the nursing curriculum resulted in better performance on the course than those students with good aggregate points. And so it goes on. There are always likely to have been more interesting analyses, if only . . . In any case Gilbert thought it would probably have been difficult to persuade the polytechnic to release students' aggregate points scores. There is often some sensitivity about releasing applicants' entry qualifications amongst institutions and between departments – and not only in Singapore. Moreover, Gilbert's supervisor made it clear that if such detailed analysis had been undertaken, he would have been well on the way to a PhD! Enough was surely enough, so, it's perhaps as well he was not able to obtain the aggregate scores, or the MEd would never have been submitted. One thing we all learn in research is that we can't ever do everything. There are always 'What ifs' and 'if onlys'.

FURTHER READING

Bryman, A. and Cramer, D. (1994) *Quantitative Data Analysis for Social Scientists*, revised edn. London: Routledge.

Chapter 8, pp. 152–190, 'Bivariate analysis: exploring relationships', covers cross-tabulation, cross-tabulation and significance, correlation, scatter diagrams and relationships between ordinal variables – and more. Explanations are clear and helpful.

Clarke, G.M. and Cooke, D. (1992) *A Basic Course in Statistics*, 3rd edn. London: Arnold.

Chapter 20, pp. 335–8, 'Correlation', includes scatter diagrams, correlation coefficients and fallacies interpreting calculated correlation co-efficients (correlation does not imply cause). Good examples, exercises *and* answers.

Cohen, L. and Holliday, M. (1996) *Practical Statistics for Students*. London: Paul Chapman.

This is a very readable text which provides a comprehensive overview of statistical methods.

Cramer, D. (1997) *Basic Statistics for Social Research*. London: Routledge.

Chapter 9, pp. 250–76, 'Tests of association for categorical and ordinal data', is thorough, though it certainly helps to have a little statistical knowledge. Covers, among other things, Kendall's tau a, b and c (pp. 245–61), discussion of when these tests are appropriate and the associated formulae.

McMillan, J.H. and Schumacher, S. (1984) *Research in Education – A Conceptual Introduction*. Boston, MA: Little, Brown.

This is rather dated now, but is still a useful text which covers a wide range of general issues concerning educational research and details on statistics.

Moore, D. (1997) *Statistics, Concepts and Controversies*. New York, NY: Freeman.

Another useful text which offers numerous examples of data analysis. Chapter 4, on presenting data clearly, is particularly useful.

Oppenheim, A.N. (1992) *Questionnaire Design, Interviewing and Attitude Measurement*. London: Pinter.

Very useful examples of the problems of cause and effect on pages 13–20.

Punch, K.F. (1998) *Introduction to Social Research: Quantitative and Qualitative Approaches*. London: Sage.

Pages 51–6 provide a succinct, easy to read account of problems associated with causation and the care which needs to be taken claiming cause and effect.

Sapsford, R. and Abbott, P. (1996) 'Ethics, politics and research', in R. Sapsford, and V. Jupp, *Data Collection and Analysis*. London: Sage.

Part IV, Chapter 13, 'Ethics and research', pp. 318–22, provides excellent guidelines, particularly their definition of 'confidentiality' and 'anonymity'.

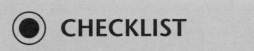
CHECKLIST

1 Select a general area of interest.	Don't be in too much of a hurry to decide. Second or third choices might be better.
2 Make sure you obtain permission to carry out your study from your institution or organization, and consult the ethics code, if any.	Many have strict rules about conditions under which research is allowed to take place.
3 Give as much time as you can afford to review relevant literature.	That will not only tell you about other research in your area of interest. It may also give you ideas about how to structure your own research.
4 Consult colleagues about feasibility.	You may well need their help as the research proceeds.
5 Produce first-thoughts research questions.	Order and wording are not important at this stage.
6 Refine and focus your research questions.	Always go back to 'What am I trying to find out'?
7 Move to specific questions.	These will form the basis of your research, so these questions need to be very precise.
8 Draw boundaries.	You will be working to a strict time limit. You can't do everything, so be realistic about what you can do.

9 Concepts aren't observable, so they have to be transposed into indicators.	All quantitative research has to be measurable, so think about that when you are selecting variables. Different types of variable can present different analytical challenges.
10 Begin the process of establishing a conceptual framework and begin to consider groupings.	The framework may need to be adapted as the research develops, but it's good to have a shot at it as early as possible. Sort out your bins!
11 Decide on the best ways of obtaining the answers you need.	You can't begin to think about *how* you can collect your data until you are finally satisfied you know *what* you are trying to find out. Methods follow from questions.
12 Decide on and begin to design your data-collecting instruments.	Pilot them carefully, take note of feedback and make any adjustments to wording, structure and layout. You will need several drafts.
13 Clear the drafts, if necessary, with any vetting committees.	The committee may have good ideas, but in any case, if the rules of the house say you have to obtain final clearance before distribution, you have to do it.
14 Go back again to 'What do I want to find out?' just in case you have strayed. Consider which methods of collecting the data are likely to provide answers.	Ask for guidance. Your supervisor should be able to help, but if not will know who can.

15	Select and design data-collecting instruments.	Make sure you pilot them thoroughly and take account of feedback.
16	Try out analytical strategies before you decide finally on your data-collecting instruments.	Remember that it is always important to understand which statistical applications will provide you with the data you need.
17	If you are looking for relationships between variables, you may need to consider correlational techniques.	Make sure you read about and understand what they are, what they will do – and what they won't do.
18	If you are thinking about using a computer statistical package, don't wait until you are ready to begin your analysis.	Sounds obvious, but . . . Make sure you find out early in the research what computer facilities and support your institution has; ask if software is available for installation into your home computer; find out whose job it is to advise about programs; allocate plenty of time to familiarize yourself with the complexities of your computer *and* of the package.
19	Select a computer program which suits your requirements, key in the responses, look at the results, select which you wish to include in your dissertation and decide what are the best ways of presenting the results (tables, bar charts, histograms etc.) in ways which will make the implications of the data clear.	It is unlikely everything which emerges from your computer will be worth including so be selective. Don't clutter up your dissertation with statements of the obvious unless there are good reasons for doing so. Findings will require interpretation and explanation.

| 20 If you find you are suffering from the 'giving up syndrome', take a deep breath and carry on. You've done too much work to give up now. | Sunshine days are bound to come. |

Part 3

THE EXPERIMENTAL STUDY

Developing the research topic • literature review • obtaining permission • ethical dilemmas in experimental research • computer based learning (CBL) • aims of the study • independent and dependent variables • control and experimental groups • ethical dilemmas of experimental research • the CBL support package • WinEcon • hypotheses • the mean • t-tests • t-distribution • level of significance • p values • interviews • observation • results • discussion • commentary • recommendations • discussion.

3.1

BACKGROUND TO
THE STUDY

This MEd study was carried out by Lim Cher Ping who at the time was teaching in a college in Singapore (Lim 1997). Like most other new researchers whose work we are considering in this book, he was registered for this part-time degree at a British university. He had a statistics and IT background and so had a head start over most of the researchers whose work we are discussing. He did not have to learn how to use a computer, which is what Helen had to do and was not in the least 'afraid of stats' as Gilbert claimed to be. He had no trouble dealing with computer statistical packages but he was, nevertheless, new to research. He had always tried to make a note of what went well with his teaching and what required some amendment, but he had reached the stage of wanting to adopt a more formal approach to research on his own practice, to experience the discipline of becoming a practitioner researcher and to be able to relate theory to practice. The importance of this topic became of even greater significance when the Singapore government's Masterplan for IT in Education was announced (the web page address of the plan is provided in the References at the end of the book: Masterplan for IT in Singapore (2001)). This was an investment of two billion Singapore dollars to make learning with computers a way of life in the classroom and involved the production of a six-year plan for education, designed to meet the challenges of the twenty-first century. The intention was that by the end of this period, all 360 schools in Singapore would be using computers in unprecedented ways – 'to plan, teach, assess and reach out to one another as well as the world' (*Straits Times*, 1997: 1). Although the Singapore Ministry of Education was to take responsibility for supporting services and for providing a basic framework for the integration of IT into schools, responsibility for the management of IT was to rest with the schools. This inevitably posed major challenges for schools which had to integrate the new innovations into their strategic plans. From experience, Cher Ping knew that in the rush of development which always surrounds new technology, the importance of the context in which it is to be used is rarely considered and yet he believed context to be of supreme importance.

His research topic began to emerge from

- the knowledge that fundamental changes in the curriculum would be required as a result of the government's six-year plan;
- his belief that an educational package can only be evaluated in its own learning situation; and
- knowledge that he would be teaching A level Economics to the so-called remedial classes in his junior college.

We should perhaps mention at this point that his college had high entry requirements. Students were selected from the top 10 per cent of the O level cohort who had also exhibited superior performance across a wide range of endeavour, especially academic, so the notion of 'remedial' may be rather different from that in other, non-selective educational institutions in the world. However, the problem of underachievement still exists, even in the most high-flying schools, colleges and universities. Cher Ping was convinced that the problem with his 'remedial' classes was not so much that students were slow but rather that they lacked motivation. Many were just not able to see the relevance of Economics. They found it impractical and boring because the 'what if' questions which are central to Economics can't be explored as easily as might be the case in a scientific experiment. He resolved to adopt a different approach from the traditional textbook, lecture and discussion methods which were apparently proving ineffective. His alternative approach was to integrate computers within his remedial classes and to let the students learn at their own pace. He hoped the approach might help to initiate the students into thinking like economists and facilitate the acquisition of the important cognitive skills required for effective economic analysis and evaluation.

He decided his dissertation would be an evaluation of the use of computer-based learning (CBL) as a support for underachieving Economics students, with the emphasis of the research being on the context rather than the multimedia products themselves. But before he could move into the actual planning stage of his research, he had to find out if anyone had been involved in similar research before and, if so, when, where and whether any conclusions had been drawn which were relevant to his own situation.

3.2

THE LITERATURE REVIEW

Cher Ping's early extensive reading of published literature on the topic of CBL from Singapore, Australia, the USA and the UK was, in his view, crucial because he considered that 'you have to be theoretically sound before you can move on to designing methods and collecting data'. He was perhaps fortunate in that he had library access to the British Council in Singapore, the National University of Singapore and the National Institute of Education of Singapore. He made use of all their facilities.

He proved to be an exceptionally well focused reader in finding out all he could about the impact of CBL on student learning. He was disciplined in his reading, wrote notes on how he felt about what he had read, how some of the findings might be of interest for his dissertation and whether the ideas were useful or, in his view, total nonsense. As he went on, themes began to emerge as they always do and he began to group findings under headings. More literature emerged during the course of the research, but by the time he had finished the main part of the preliminary reading, his literature review was as good as finished. It only needed to be tinkered with later on. That in our view is admirable but rarely achieved. All supervisors will advise research students to work systematically in this way but the personal discipline involved is considerable and not all can resist the temptation to read indiscriminately in the hope that the next journal article or the next book will provide the solution to all problems. He had discovered that

> Many research students seem to think you can just read and read and read and after reading 50 articles you can then start writing, but that doesn't work. That's too late. By that time, you've forgotten what the first 10 articles were about.

Before he began his reading, he had thought it possible that his underachieving students might be lacking in certain aspects of the cognitive domain which made it difficult for them to understand the more complex conceptual areas of Economics, to learn material to a deeper level and understand more connections among concepts. He was looking for clues as to whether this might be true and, if so, whether any CBL packages had been successful in addressing this particular problem.

From the early days of his reading, he was looking for patterns, themes and possibilities. He had his own ideas, though realized there were likely to be many changes and adjustments before he felt sufficiently confident to settle on a satisfactory framework. His reading enabled him to identify various categories associated with the effectiveness of CBL as a support to learning in terms of

- *achievement of learning outcomes*, with subsections covering the achievement of higher level objectives, namely knowledge, understanding, application, analysis, synthesis and evaluation (Bloom, 1956: 3);
- *student satisfaction and motivation*;
- *development–cost ratios*;
- *redeployment of staff*; and
- *flexibility*.

He knew that those categories would be interdependent but the grouping of findings under these headings enabled him to provide structure to his analysis of previous research. There is no doubt that his early determination to write and comment on each article and each book as he read enabled him to think in terms of analytical structures at an early stage.

His review ran to about 7000 words, none of which was superfluous, though even the most demanding of examiners would have been content with somewhat less detail. However, the extent and detail of his reading enabled him to examine claims which were made in the literature for enhanced learning through CBL, which were that it provided students with

- the medium to understand complex concepts and so provide a framework for thinking;
- the ability to study materials to a deeper level and understand more connections among concepts;
- the ability to understand and retain a whole range of issues more clearly and so be less intimidated by examination questions;

There were also claims in the literature that CBL had:

- promoted learner autonomy;
- improved student motivation;
- provided students with tasks that were personally meaningful and challenging to them; and,
- demonstrated that students became more engaged in the learning process, enjoyed the whole experience of CBL and participated enthusiastically.

His findings gave him confidence that CBL can, in the right circumstances, provide a context in which economic theories can be embedded and used by students, and that it can enhance Economics education – *as long as* it is incorporated into the teaching scheme in such a way as to provide a valid contribution to an overall sound teaching strategy. In short, it needed to be planned in ways that enhance students' confidence and their ability to succeed; enable them to move from a teacher-led, passive student role to a student-centred, active student role, from knowing *what* to knowing *how*; and from working alone to working in small groups.

He did not anticipate the outcomes of his research would initiate big changes, such as a shift from topic-based to problem-based learning, or the abandonment of lectures in favour of other learning activities, but he did feel it might promote small and local evolutionary adaptations of CBL and highlight ways in which the curriculum might be influenced and adapted as a result of IT development. That seemed a worthwhile outcome to Cher Ping, and it seemed good enough to us.

His review of the literature had provided him with a good theoretical base. He was clear about the limitations of his research and he was ready to move on.

3.3

OBTAINING PERMISSION
AND ETHICAL DILEMMAS
IN EXPERIMENTAL
RESEARCH

As always, he had to obtain permission to carry out his study. In Singapore, even though the government actively encourages other forms of assessment, examination results are still of supreme importance and any threat to good results would certainly have been unacceptable. The most common college strategy for addressing the problems of underachieving students was through mass lectures conducted after lessons, and the CBL proposal was far removed from that approach. However, the principal gave very positive support and the only condition laid down was that what was planned did not jeopardize students' examination results. He received similar support from his head of department and from colleagues who were willing to collaborate in a variety of very positive ways. Permission was also sought and given from parents.

It's worth noting at this point that there can be ***ethical questions*** associated with ***experimental research***, which need to be considered. As Cohen *et al.* note:

This model premised on notions of isolation and control of variables in order to establish causality may be appropriate for a laboratory, though whether, in fact, a social situation ever *could become* the antiseptic, artificial world of the laboratory or *should become* such a world is both an empirical and moral question . . . Further, the ethical dilemmas of treating humans as manipulable, controllable and inanimate are considerable.

(Cohen *et al.* 2000: 212)

Quite so, though there can be ethical problems in all research, in the world of the laboratory and in the world of human beings. The social world never could become what Cohen *et al.* describe as 'the antiseptic artificial world of the laboratory', but that is not to say that no experimental research involving human beings should ever be carried out. To be aware of these ethical dilemmas is important but, as Sapsford and Abbott (1996: 318) remind us, an even stronger principle of all research ethics 'is that subjects of the research should not be *harmed* by it', and that is a principle which can never be ignored.

In any experimental study, there is always the possibility that the ***experimental group*** (sometimes referred to as the treatment group) might have an advantage over the ***control group***. Most of the published literature on CBL indicated that it had, or could have, positive effects on learning outcome, motivation, collaboration and communication. Cher Ping knew that, even if his students did not. All the students who were classified as being in need of remedial support met in combined groups and they would obviously talk and ask each other what was happening in the different groups wouldn't they? Was it fair that one group had the use of a very expensive and scarce educational resource, namely the customized WinEcon software, while the other did not?

So was the control group likely to be harmed in any way? On balance, Cher Ping thought not because all students classified as 'remedial' were given special attention, though of a different kind. The main difference between the traditional and the experimental programme was the medium of learning – a CBL support package versus traditional college remedial package. Everything possible had been done to ensure fair deals for all and after some heart-searching, he decided the research could proceed without undue anxiety about lack of equal access to computers.

3.4

AIMS AND PURPOSE OF
THE STUDY

Cher Ping's introductory paragraph to his Design and Method chapter reads as follows:

> This research study attempts to investigate the effectiveness of CBL on students' performance compared with the traditional method of remedial lessons. The question being raised is whether or not the students using CBL as part of the CBL support package benefit in terms of achievement of learning outcomes (achieving higher level objectives in Bloom's taxonomy, providing scaffolding for thinking, promoting problem-solving skills and promoting learner autonomy), higher satisfaction and motivation level, more collaboration and better communication, as compared with their counterparts who do not.

This is a tall order and not to be undertaken by the faint-hearted, but no one could accuse Cher Ping of faint-heartedness. He knew he would have to be very thorough about the way he planned his research and he decided that he would need three different approaches to data collecting, as follows:

- the establishment of two student groups (control and experimental) and statistical tests to evaluate differences between mid- and final-year grade scores of each group;
- face-to-face interviews with each member of the experimental group in order to discover their views about the CBL experience;
- observation of students' behaviour and practice when working on CBL tasks at the computer.

He needed to discover whether his CBL approach benefited students in the experimental group compared with students in the control group who were following the 'normal' curriculum for underachievers; to discover students' views about CBL; and to examine their working practice. In other words, it was necessary for him to discover whether there was any evidence of the effect of the independent variable (the use of CBL) on the dependent variable (the examination results) and students' views about their experience.

Independent and dependent variables

A quick reminder about the difference between 'independent' and 'dependent' variables.

Solomon and Winch's illustration of the hypothesized link between smoking and lung cancer makes the distinction quite clear.

> Suppose we examine the link between smoking and lung cancer. We would have two variables, the *number of cigarettes smoked* and the *incidence of lung cancer*. We are investigating whether or not smoking causes lung cancer. Nobody would seriously suggest that it is the other way round, that lung cancer causes smoking. So the incidence of cancer is *dependent* on the number of cigarettes smoked. We say that the number of cigarettes is the *independent variable* and that the incidence of cancer is the *dependent variable*.
>
> (Solomon and Winch 1994: 66)

So the use of CBL was the *independent* variable while the examination results were the *dependent* variable. We'll return to some of these issues later in this chapter, but first we'll see how he selected his two groups which had to have the same or at least very similar backgrounds if the experiment was to have any validity.

Control and experimental groups

Establishing identical groups is difficult and so researchers have to do the best they can to ensure that group members are as similar as possible. Cher Ping decided on a number of demographic and aptitude comparisons.

At the time he began his research, all the first-year A level group had completed two terms of a two-year A level Economics course at the college and had just received their mid-year examination results. Some students had not managed an E grade, an E grade being the minimum grade to warrant an A level pass – and clearly that was not good enough as far as the college authorities were concerned. Action had to be taken to ensure a better result would be achieved at the end of the two-year course and so these 'low-grade' students were deemed to be in need of a remedial programme.

He found that:

- There was no significant difference in the average household income of the two groups.
- None of the subjects engaged a private tutor or sought the help of a senior or older sibling to improve on their Economics grades.
- Aptitude indicators for the two groups were obtained from the GCE O level results. No significant group differences in aptitude were identified.
- The mean of the mid-year grade scores for students in the control group was not significantly different from the mean for students in the treatment group.

All possible variations in letter grades were converted into numeric equivalents using a 16-point scale (F = 0, 0 = 1*), E– = 2,

E = 3, E+ = 4, D– = 5, D = 6, D+ = 7, C– = 8, C = 9, C+ = 10, B– = 11, B = 12, B+ = 13, A– = 14, A = 15). A fail was taken to be either a grade F or O. (*The O grade is one level above F as the former represents a pass at GCE O level.)

Good enough? Well we certainly think it was. It could perhaps be argued that Cher Ping could have taught both groups in order to control variability of teaching though, even then, his knowledge of the selected computer package and the work of his experimental group might have influenced his teaching of the control group. Experimental researchers frequently have to face dilemmas such as this. They just have to be aware of the dangers of *bias* and do their best to prevent it in whichever ways seem best – and possible. He weighed one option against the other and decided to keep to the original plan which was that one of his colleagues would teach the control group (which was to follow the traditional remedial programme) and he would teach the experimental group (which was to follow the CBL programme).

He was anxious that any extraneous variable that might possibly influence the results should not only be controlled but be seen to be controlled. Certain measures were duly taken to do everything possible to avoid contamination.

- Both groups covered the same ground as that laid down in the A level syllabus.
- In order to ensure that no students would be handicapped or have an unfair advantage over others because of the different approach of the tutors, all students attended the same lectures.
- All tutorial questions were assigned by the lecturer responsible for the particular topic and all tutors were given the same set of suggested solutions.
- All the remedial and CBL support lessons were conducted in the same time frame and with the same scheme of work.
- Students' identities and tutorial groups were not known to the grader. Students' final grades were determined solely by their relative performance in the common examination and no credits were given for class participation.
- Both the experimental and control group were asked to work on two individual assignments and a group project per term.

Throughout the 28 weeks of study, the control group underwent the traditional approach of remedial lessons. The twice-weekly one-hour sessions included explanation of key concepts by the tutor, discussion of essay outlines, data-response questions and clarification of incorrect answers to multiple-choice questions.

The CBL support package and WinEcon

The experimental group worked through the CBL support package in groups of three. The package included expensive WinEcon software (an undergraduate interactive learning programme designed by a consortium of eight UK university Economics departments), which included websites designed to assist students with assignments and with their project; e-mail communication with the tutor and with fellow students was also included in the package. The software offered more than 75 hours of tutorial material and included self-assessment questions and examinations, economic databases, an economic glossary, references to leading economic texts – and much more. It proved to be an excellent teaching aid but, as is often the case when using externally prepared software, it had to be customized to suit college and student needs.

It was never intended to be a substitute for tutorial sessions, student–teacher and student–student discussions, notes and reference books. The misguided notion that all a teacher has to do to teach an externally produced computer package is to switch on the computers and go away for a cup of tea, or even a few cups of tea, is some distance from reality. Any teachers who have used externally produced packages will know all about that!

Cher Ping's preparation was very thorough. He had established the control and experimental group, had done everything possible to avoid bias, knew what he intended to include in his CBL support package, was familiar with the software and had adapted it for the particular needs of the students. He now felt sufficiently confident to move on to his plans for data collection and analysis.

3.5

THE PLAN FOR DATA
COLLECTION AND ANALYSIS

The statistical tests

Cher Ping was quite clear about how he intended to obtain his data. He writes:

> This investigation will be explored from several different perspectives. Average mid-year and final grade levels will be obtained for both experimental and control groups and differences between the two groups will be investigated. The analysis will address the degree of change from mid-year to final grades for each of the two groups . . . and findings will be submitted to two sample t-tests with unequal ns to evaluate differences between means for each group.

He selected *t-tests* because he wished to find out whether the difference between the two means was sufficiently large to suggest that it was not due to chance and because they were suitable for dealing with his small sample where the numbers (ns) in the groups did not necessarily have to be the same (there were 11 in the control group and 9 in the experimental group).

The *hypotheses*

Denscombe reminds us that

> Researchers using the t-test take the null hypothesis as their
> starting point. They presume that there is no real difference
> until they can be persuaded otherwise by a statistical test
> which tells them that there is a very strong likelihood that
> any variations found between the two sets of data were the
> result of something other than pure chance.
>
> (Denscombe 1998: 201)

Two hypotheses were constructed, the first of which (H_1) stated
that, in terms of examination results,

> The students in the experimental group improve more than
> the students in the control group.

This hypothesis, expressed in algebraic terms, becomes H_1: $\mu_e > \mu_c$
(μ is the Greek letter normally used to indicate 'mean', the sub-
script 'e' represents the experimental group and 'c' the control
group. So the formula states that the *mean* of the mid-year and
final grade levels of the treatment group will be greater than the
mean of the mid-year and the final grade levels of the control
group). The mean is calculated by dividing the sum of the values
by the total number of values.

The ***null hypothesis*** (H_0) states that, in terms of examination
results,

> There is no significant difference between students in the
> experimental and the control group.

Expressed in algebraic form, this is H_0: $\mu_e = \mu_c$ which states that
the mean of the mid-year and final grade levels of the experimental group will be the same as the mean of the control group.
The wording of hypotheses has to be precise because not only do
they predict the relationship between two or more events but
they also indicate the data needed for the testing to take place

(see Greene and D'Oliveira 1982: 7 and Rose and Sullivan 1996: 168, 239, 243).

As we have seen, Cher Ping made vigorous efforts to ensure that, as far as possible, the groups were similar and so if the mean of the grade levels of the experimental group proved to be higher than those of the control group, it might be inferred that the CBL programme produced the difference. However, it wasn't enough for him to know that the mean of the test scores of one group was higher than the other. He needed to know whether it was *significantly* higher.

T-tests are about probabilities, not certainties, and he had to decide on **probability (p) levels** before carrying out the tests. The p level is the probability that results will not have arisen by chance. The smaller the p value, the more reliable the result. The level chosen is completely arbitrary but, by convention, most significance (probability) levels will be likely to be set at or around five times in a hundred ($p < 0.05$). However, he set the level at one in a hundred ($p < 0.01$) as the criterion for significance/non-significance which no doubt reflected his CBL experience, together with the findings in the related published literature.

We shall consider some of the results of these tests in Chapter 6 but, before then, we need to see what plans he had for collecting data from the interviews and observations.

The interviews

Although he was perfectly at ease with the quantitative part of the research, Cher Ping was less comfortable with the qualitative part and with his role as interviewer. In spite of his anxiety, he felt it was essential to carry out face-to-face interviews with each member of the experimental group in order to ensure that, as far as possible, he had their personal and honest opinions about the Economics support lessons which he thought might be different from his own.

He was particularly concerned about the likelihood of interview bias and that, because of his inexperience as an interviewer, he might involuntarily 'lead' his interviewees. He was also uneasy about what he saw as the possibility of inaccurate data because he thought students might omit information or fall into the trap of selective recall if they thought he was looking for certain responses. His concerns sent him back to the literature, and his reading led him to believe that his best approach would be to prepare open-ended questions which he hoped would give him the chance of probing responses, clearing up any misunderstandings and allowing him to make a truer assessment of what the respondents really believed. In principle, that seemed to be sound, though it was clear that it would be more difficult to code and quantify data from open-ended questions than from structured questions, and that worried him.

With the participants' consent, he decided to tape the interviews which would relieve him of the burden of trying to make notes of responses and so give him the opportunity of noting any non-verbal signals on the spot. After the interviews, he anticipated he would then be able to listen to the tapes, look for common themes, individual variations and any emerging contextualization of themes. He tried out interviews with other student groups, took note of their feedback and made adjustments to his interview schedule which he decided should include students' views on

- whether their performance in Economics had improved as a result of their use of the CBL support package;
- whether it had helped them to understand economic concepts and theories;
- which aspect of the Economics course they considered had been most effectively taught by the CBL package (if any);
- the extent to which they found CBL met their needs as learners (if so, in what way?);
- whether their experience of using the Internet for project and assignments was practical (if so, how?);
- whether they found cooperative working with their group or classmates helpful (if not, what went wrong?);
- how they saw the teacher's role in a CBL environment.

He also needed to know how they coped when they were working at the computer on CBL tasks and the only way he could find out was by observing them.

The observations

In his original time plan, a maximum of an hour and a half was allowed for audio-recording students' individual or group **verbal behaviour** (asking questions, receiving answers, agreeing, disagreeing and giving explanations). The **non-verbal behaviour** which was observed by one of Cher Ping's colleagues was to include keyboard entries and mutual keyboard use. He was only interested in academic, task-oriented behaviour and what were considered to be relevant items were specified before the observations took place.

He knew there might be problems with such a structured observation and that the categories might be so rigid as to overlook other important behaviour but it seemed to him to be better for the observer to know exactly what he was looking for than to be trying to note anything and everything in case it came in handy – and we agree.

* * *

Once all plans were made, statistical tests, interview and observation schedules tried out and trial analysis completed, he was ready to move into the data-collecting stage of his research. So what did he discover?

3.6

THE RESULTS

The statistical tests

There was an increase in grades between mid-year and final examinations for both groups, though the control group improvement was not as dramatic as for the experimental group. The results demonstrated that students in the control group improved their mean grades from mid-year to final grade by 2.45 grade scale points while students in the experimental group improved by an average of 5.67 grade score points. 2.45 and 5.67 are the t-values calculated statistically from the two means, the probability of the results occurring by chance being less than one in a hundred.

The null hypothesis (H_o) predicted that there would be no significant difference between the scores of the two groups and as that proved not to be the case, Cher Ping was able to reject the null hypothesis. Of the three students who began the CBL support programme with a failing grade, all three ended their first-year course by bringing their grades up to at least an A level pass. The six students who started the support programme with only a bare GCE A level pass grade also brought their grades up by at least two grade scale points.

Three students in the control group failed to receive at least an A level pass and two students showed no improvement in their grades.

These statistics are complex and though there are computer statistical packages which will do the calculations for you, you still have to understand what you are doing, why, and what the printouts mean. If you are a relatively inexperienced researcher and have only a modest mathematical background, you will need to find out whose job it is in your institution to give advice to research students. Ask for advice, read as much as you can about t-tests, t-distributions, degrees of freedom – and then check you are making the right decisions. We provide sources of further reading at the end of this Part and in the glosssary that discuss some of the principles involved. However, before we move on to consider what Cher Ping found from his interviews and observations, we'll leave you with Greene and D'Oliveira's reminder about choosing statistical tests. They write that

The first and most important point we want to emphasize is this: *the selection of an appropriate statistical test follows from the experimental design you have chosen to test your hypothesis.* Once you have made these decisions you will find that you have automatically selected which statistical test to use for analysing the significance of your experimental data.

(Greene and D'Oliveira 1982: 35)

Right. So if your preparation is sufficiently thorough, your hypotheses well devised and methods of data collection carefully selected, then the test selection will take care of itself.

The interviews

Interviews were held with all nine members of the experimental group and responses to the questions revealed generally positive attitudes towards CBL in the learning of Economics. In response to the question 'Has the CBL package helped in the understanding of economic concepts and theories?' the following opinions were typical of the group as a whole:

Student A: It's very difficult for me to pick up information that I cannot clearly apply to something. Microecon and Macroecon are frustrating because they seem to be a mass of garbled concepts that must be memorized for tests. CBL has allowed me to see these concepts as tools for solving problems.

Student B: The computer enables formulae, tables of numbers and graphs to be linked readily. Before the CBL support classes, I could not see the relationship between total cost, average cost and marginal cost. WinEcon has allowed me to see the connections between them by changing one representation and seeing changes in others.

The question 'Have you found cooperative working relationships with your fellow group members to be useful?' produced mainly positive responses on the lines of the views expressed by Students A, B and C:

Student C: My group worked well together. My group members helped me to learn and understand economic concepts much better. Whenever I was in doubt, my questions would be answered by one member of the group. Otherwise, we would work at it together and talk the concepts over. As far as possible, we try to sort out the problems among ourselves. I guess it's much clearer for a student to explain to a student rather than a teacher explaining to a student. We students can talk on the same wavelength. Besides academic support, we provided each other with emotional support as well.

Only one student (Student D) said she had not enjoyed cooperative working in her group, though her complaints centred on personal relationship problems with the other members of the group rather than with the CBL programme. She recalled that

Initially, things were bad. The other two members seemed to disagree with everything I said. Both of them would be at the keyboard, viewing websites and software at their own pace . . . I was always the outsider. I was never part of their discussions and I usually ended up day-dreaming. After the fifth lesson, I told them off. They've been trying to accommodate me ever since . . . everything was still pretty superficial but at least I am no longer 'unseen' and 'unheard'. Although I've benefited from these CBL support lessons, I think I prefer to work alone.

Cher Ping had been anxious to discover how students saw the teacher's role in a CBL environment. Most of them said they noticed a distinct change in the role of the teacher as compared to the traditional lecture/tutorial system. They saw the teacher 'less as an information dispenser and more as a guide', 'less as an authoritative expert', 'more as a fellow learner who shares information with the others' and 'no longer as the fountainhead of information and knowledge'. The interviews produced interesting information about students' views of the CBL programme and of his role as guide rather than teacher.

The observations

Peer tutoring

One of the most interesting outcomes of the observations was that in most cases it was clear that students were willing to work cooperatively and to provide peer tutoring. They were very active in asking questions and giving answers and, on average, one question was asked every 2.5 minutes.

The following example was typical of much of the peer tutoring observed:

Student A: Can the demand curve be upward sloping (pointing at the graph on the screen)?
Student B: Yes, when it doesn't abide by the Law of Demand.
Student A: What kind of goods are we looking at?
Student C: Possibly ostentatious goods.

In addition to the question asking and answering, students nearly always (95 per cent of the time observed) received explanations from each other in response to questions.

Student B: I still don't understand how an increase in money supply leads to inflation (after looking at the raw data on the computer screen).

Student A: Remember what we did under the Quantity Theory of Money?

Student B: Vaguely.

Student C: Why investment increase?

Student A: When money supply increases, interest rates will fall. With the fall in interest rates, investment will increase.

Student C: Why investment increase?

Student A: Producers want to maximize profits. With a low interest rate, cost of investment falls and thus more investment.

Student B: That's right. And with that increase in investment, aggregate demand will increase and so general price level will start to rise. If this is sustained, then there'll be inflation.

Student C: I remember now . . . should we go back to that topic in WinEcon where the graphs are presented?

Students A and B agreed and soon the group was studying the graphs flashed on the computer screen.

So, the peer tutoring appeared to be very successful but there can be problems, not least the possibility of answers being wrong. It's not possible for a tutor (or an observer) to hear everything that's going on in the groups all the time but Cher Ping was aware of the possibility of misinformation and had implemented a system of monitoring work and regular review sessions. Without those safeguards, some of the potential dangers could have been real.

Mutual keyboard usage

Mutual keyboard usage referred to those times when students in the groups were using the keyboard to answer a single question. It signified a form of on-task engagement as they were expected to agree an answer before typing it into the computer. So verbal

exchange was encouraged since all members of the group participated in answering the question.

The observer (Cher Ping's colleague) noted that students were
working with confidence. They found the computer-based tasks
to be really exciting. This was observed particularly when they
were surfing the net to complete projects. They clearly took pride
in being able to use the same computer-based tools as employed
by economists.

3.7

OVERALL FINDINGS

You will recall that Cher Ping's study of published research into the effectiveness of CBL made claims which he categorized under the following headings:

1 Achievement of learning outcomes (with subsections covering the achievement of higher level objectives, namely knowledge, understanding, application, analysis, synthesis and evaluation (Bloom 1956: 3).
2 Student satisfaction and motivation.
3 Development–cost ratios.
4 Redeployment of staff.
5 Flexibility.

For the analysis and discussion of his own data, he decided to select only three main categories, with associated subgroups, which covered most of the above items, but which suited his data analysis better. They were the CBL support package and

1 achievement of learning outcomes (achievement of higher level objectives in Bloom's taxonomy; provision of scaffolding for thinking and promotion of problem-solving skills; promotion of learner autonomy);

2 meeting the needs of students as learners (relevance to real life; fast feedback; teamwork; communication and enjoyment);
3 development–cost ratios.

It's not possible for us to do justice to his discussion of findings, nor to provide information about ways in which he related his own findings to the published literature on CBL, but we shall at least do our best to provide a skeleton outline of the evidence he reports. We'll start with the achievement of learning outcomes.

The CBL support package and the achievement of learning outcomes

Achievement of higher level objectives in Bloom's taxonomy

He knew from the start of his research that he wished to face up to this very difficult area and he was well aware of the problems which faced him. However, he was not one to reject a challenge. His three-pronged approach to data collection was sound and, when all the data had been analysed, he had some confidence that much of the improvement in students' achievement of higher level objectives could be attributed to the effect of the CBL support package. He writes:

> Because analysis, synthesis and evaluation are most difficult to teach and because conventional teaching techniques are least suitable for higher level learning objectives, they tend to be underemphasized in the A level Economics course. However, based on the significant improvement in the experimental group as compared to the control group, CBL in support classes has been shown to assist the low-performance students in efficiently moving up Bloom's hierarchy of learning. After using the WinEcon software, these students not only managed to understand the interrelationships between theories, but were also able to apply them to various 'real world' situations.

He discovered that discussing quite complex empirical studies was much easier if students had struggled with simple data-handling problems provided by the software. The observations revealed that they were able to analyse and reorganize data gathered from the Internet and were able to see how theories fitted into a larger context which enabled them to understand certain theories that were not previously recognized. His findings also confirmed some of the claims made in the literature regarding the importance of asking questions, providing answers and explanations at the computer.

Explanations are believed to signify a higher level of cognitive processing which can benefit the students who gave the explanation and those who received it, which might have contributed to their performance in the final examination.

Provision of a framework for thinking

TheWinEcon software presented students with an initial series of rule frames which provided a definition of concepts, lists of steps in the procedure and statements of the relationship between concepts. It allowed students who regarded Economics as 'a mass of garbled concepts that must be learnt for tests' to see, understand and apply the appropriate rule for a specific object or event. Formulae, tables of numbers and graphs could be readily linked and it became obvious from Cher Ping's interviews and observation that they could see the effects of changing variables almost immediately.

He was pleased to have discovered that the instructional design of WinEcon provided them 'with the cognitive structures necessary for dealing with abstract environmental relationships'.

Promotion of problem-solving skills

Results from the face-to-face interviews with the experimental group demonstrated that the support package not only helped students to acquire knowledge and communication of ideas but it also improved their problem-solving skills by providing them with a more in-depth understanding of economic concepts. He writes:

> One group of students identified inflation as a problem. They first gathered and studied the background factors based on the data they had collected. They then brainstormed for potential solutions. Their understanding of the types and causes of inflation and the Philips Curve enabled them to evaluate the consequences of each potential solution. A solution was then decided using cost-benefit analysis.

Problem solving is a creative process which demands much more than the simple application of previously learned rules. The approach of the CBL support programme exposed students to various economic problems which they had not previously encountered, based on the real-world data they collected. They were then expected to suggest solutions to the identified problems and to apply the most appropriate solutions. From the evidence of the interviews and the observations, there would seem to be little doubt that this approach helped to develop their problem-solving skills.

Promotion of learner autonomy

As we have reported earlier, in the CBL support class, the control of learning had shifted from the teacher to the learner, *but in a way which was determined by the teacher*. Students reported positively on this approach. The culture of the experimental group began to be dominated by the search for explanation, justification and proof of various concepts and theories discussed in class. Even though students were given responsibility for their own learning, they still needed to be taught how to handle the CBL package. For example, they needed to be taught various skills such as

- how to run the system, knowing what connects to where and with which plug, how to switch things on, which buttons to press and how to log on;

- how to navigate through the package;
- how to acquire the skills of investigation;
- how to reflect on the CBL experience; and
- how to acquire handling skills.

There was no question of the teacher leaving the group for a rest, to do a bit of shopping, or to have numerous cups of tea! Students were only able to reap the benefits of learner autonomy once those skills were acquired and the teacher's role in that process was crucial.

Meeting the needs of students as learners

Cher Ping's findings made clear that the CBL support package had many characteristics which met the needs of students as learners.

Relevance to real life

Student responses to the interview questions demonstrated that CBL used in the study met the need of most students who wanted the course to be related to what they saw as pressing economic and social issues. It helped them to illustrate the practical application of theories and the relationship between theories and real-world situations which gave them a chance to 'stop thinking like students and start thinking like economists' and to 'do' economics rather than to watch how it was done.

He had always believed that one of the problems of under-achievement was more likely to be lack of motivation rather than lack of ability and his findings provided clear evidence that this was so. He discovered that

> Students' motivation was clearly enhanced as their learning experience became more purposeful and that might account for the improvement in examination grades. They were more motivated to learn economic theories and had a more complete grasp of the theories that were covered which gave

them the edge over the control group in handling examination questions. CBL taught them how to apply theories, use evidence and reorganize.

It was clear that WinEcon was a good teaching and learning aid and it worked well with students in the experimental group who demonstrated that they enjoyed and learnt from the interactive nature of the tasks and the tutorials. However, it was not the only component in the CBL support programme, which included tutorials, attendance at lectures provided for all remedial Economics students and participation in Cher Ping's revision, feedback and review sessions.

Fast feedback

When feedback is delivered as soon as possible after the completion of a task, it becomes a powerful reinforcer. WinEcon did more than inform students that their response was correct or incorrect. When incorrect responses were made, it also provided the explanation for the correct response and it became clear that 'it was OK to be wrong'. The package opened up possibilities for conjecturing and taking a risk. Because feedback was provided continuously (rather than just at the end of the module), it reinforced the positives rather than the negatives *and focused on how performance could be improved in the future* rather than dwelling on the past.

It was apparent from the interviews and from the observations that the speed of feedback and the positive tone of the software worked well for the experimental group.

Teamwork

It was obvious, again from the interviews and observations, that CBL encouraged and supported collaborative learning. Working in small groups, students were forced to interact with fellow students. They picked up ideas from one another, or helped each other to remember things. As we saw in the quotations in the

Observations section, when they faced a problem, they talked about it and that helped them to think about the problem more clearly. All that had a positive effect on the level of achievement for most students, though not all. You'll recall that one student found the small group experience to be alienating and she preferred in future to work alone, but certainly for all other students in the group the approach worked well.

Communication

Cher Ping considered that human interaction was a primary need and that motivation was likely to be maintained if that need were satisfied. In a traditional classroom, such interaction is usually confined to exchanges between teacher and students but students in the experimental group reported an increase in teacher–student discussion via email which they considered provided a non-threatening environment. They no longer felt embarrassed to ask questions or discuss certain Economics issues with the teacher, and emailing provided students who were normally quiet in class and tutorial groups with an environment where they could ask questions, confident that their colleagues would not know about their concerns. Overall, both they and Cher Ping found that email served as an effective outreach communication, increased interaction among students and between him and individuals and, as one student said, 'it provided a safe environment for learning' which, in its turn, increased motivation.

Enjoyment

Students were asked in the interviews which of the various teaching techniques they preferred and which, in their view, contributed to their learning. The CBL package topped the ranking, with tutorial sessions being the least popular. They spoke of attractive modes of delivery and self-paced study. They felt engaged, were forced to accept responsibility for their own learning, which they came to enjoy, and the majority considered that their learning was enhanced.

The development–cost ratios

As indicated above, students' experience of the CBL support package has suggested that there are substantial benefits to be gained. However, critics of CBL may perceive the costs to be disproportionately large. There are costs in the development of any new course, including books and the production of lecture notes, but the critics' main objections generally centre on the cost of the software and the time needed to customize it. They have a point.

The WinEcon software was developed over a period of three years by the Teaching and Learning Technology Programme (TLTP) Economics Consortium and funded by the UK Higher Education Funding Council. It was estimated that its development took 40 person years of effort, involved 35 economic content authors and 17 programmers, cost in the region of £10m sterling and, at the time Cher Ping submitted his dissertation, was still undergoing revisions. As far as he was concerned, it was futile to attempt to cost the software. However, teachers' time costs are another matter. They have to review, explore and become familiar with the software and to adapt it for their own purposes. They need to prepare questions and guidelines to guide group discussion and to surf the Internet in order to obtain a compilation of the relevant websites for use in students' research. As with lectures and tutorials, once the start-up time cost of preparing the support package has been incurred, the next preparation takes far less time but even fine tuning takes time.

In Cher Ping's view, judgement of the costs and benefits of CBL should lie with an evaluation of each teacher's skills, evidence of students' improved academic performance and their enhanced learning, but all educational institutions have to work to a budget and, in hard times, that can mean that, regardless of the success of CBL schemes, neither the software nor the increased load on teachers can be afforded.

3.8

LIMITATIONS OF THE STUDY AND RECOMMENDATIONS

Cher Ping cautions that care should be taken in interpreting the results of his research. First, he points out that the sample size is very small and that might have affected both the reliability and validity of the research. However, as we have seen, in order to ensure more reliable results, the analysis was submitted to a t-test with a small p value. The level of significance was kept low at 1 per cent which gave 99 per cent probability that the results had not arisen by chance.

Second, he points out that there was always the possibility that improvement in academic results might have been due to the novelty effect which might soon wear off.

Third, only students from four Science classes in the college participated in the study and it would be difficult to generalize or even relate the research results to Arts and Commerce students who might experience a higher level of computer anxiety.

Fourth, the research only *suggested* that CBL in support classes had a positive impact on students' cognitive and attitudinal gains. It overlooked the teacher's attitudes towards the use of CBL as a teaching tool. The fact that certain pedagogical features appeal to students is no guarantee that a particular technique will be attractive to teachers because of the demands made on teaching time. Additional research would be needed before educators and software developers could fully understand the effect of CBL on Economics education.

He adds what he considers to be a fifth limitation, which is that the study was never meant to initiate big improvements such as a shift from topic-based to problem-based learning or the abandonment of lectures in favour of other learning activities. He had made it quite clear at the start of his investigation that it was more likely to promote small and local evolutionary adaptations, not revolutionary advances. That seems to us to be perfectly reasonable, is certainly not a limitation and in no way diminishes the importance of the study.

* * *

Three major recommendations were made which covered physical resource management, human resource management and collaboration among teachers and other organizations.

Physical resource management recommendations centred on the need to place equipment where it is most likely to be used (including setting up tutorial classrooms with network access points which might involve extensive alterations to the college; providing computer notebooks and accessories and increased software allowance – and more).

Human resource management covered the training of teachers in the use of IT and ongoing staff development.

Collaboration among teachers and other organizations included recommendations for teachers to work collaboratively in order to share in customizing software. Cher Ping admits that the time and effort needed to design a successful CBL support package is formidable and by sharing knowledge and experience time and effort would be put to optimal use.

Recommendations for future research covered areas such as more investigations into the effect of CBL in classrooms; development of the processes of change, integration and utilization; investigating long-term cognitive, personal and social outcomes as a result of CBL treatment which might enhance the reliability of the results; research on the outcome of teacher technology training; and, finally, further research into the blending of CBL and co-operative learning approaches in terms of their impact in specific content areas with students of different ages and social groups.

 **3.9**

DISCUSSION

Cher Ping's dissertation was of the highest quality but it was not achieved merely because he had a statistics background and so was not overfaced by the fact that he had to carry out statistical tests. It was because his preparation was sufficiently thorough to carry him through all the numerous stages of the project. Let's just consider again how he set about and carried through this task.

- For a start, he was keenly interested in his topic, really wanted to be involved in his own practitioner research and to obtain evidence, if possible, that computer-based learning had a place in the school curriculum. He refocused the topic several times before he was sufficiently confident he knew where he was going.
- This was his first attempt at research and he knew he needed a sound theoretical background before he could begin. That meant that he had to inform himself about what research on or related to his topic had been done before. He read widely, wrote up his comments immediately after reading each item and was on the lookout for key words, categories and possible themes. Inevitably many of these changed as the research progressed, but from the start he had a system and an index. He knew where to find his sources and how to adjust the

categories. You will recall that when he finished the first phase of his research, the first draft of his review of the literature was almost complete. He was fortunate in having good access to libraries and resource centres and he made good use of them.

- Carefully worded hypotheses were established, appropriate methods of data collection and possible methods of analysis considered and instruments designed and piloted.
- He understood the properties of null hypotheses and which statistical tests would be appropriate.
- He was quite happy with the statistical part of his research, but less so with the qualitative part. He had never been involved with interviews and observations before and so went back to the books, again consulted the published literature and colleagues who had previously carried out qualitative investigations.
- He worked at question wording, devised interview and observation schedules, piloted them with other groups and with colleagues and made changes where necessary. He was anxious about his inexperience in qualitative techniques and so decided to tape record interviews, with participants' permission, in order to avoid problems of taking notes on the spot and to enable him to go through the tapes later in order to identify any recurring themes. One of his colleagues agreed to carry out the observations and he and Cher Ping designed an observation checklist.
- All the data collecting was carried out, responses recorded and rough drafts produced within the original time plan.
- The limitations of the study were acknowledged.
- He did his best to write up various sections as he went along and though the final draft of the dissertation was still time-consuming and difficult, his early drafts gave him a head start over researchers who started with a blank page.
- He made no claims he could not substantiate and his recommendations and proposals for further research were sound.
- Even though English is not Cher Ping's first language, the quality of his writing and presentation was excellent.

We asked whether carrying out his research at a distance presented any problems. Would he have preferred having a tutor closer to home? He didn't think distance had bothered him too much because email contact with his supervisor was good.

> I could email thoughts and drafts to him and generally he replied quickly. He didn't bother me all the time and that suited me because I'm a very independent worker. I was able to go at my own pace and that's OK as long as you can learn on your own.

He would have liked more contact with fellow research students but he was fortunate in having colleagues to talk to. Some of them already had Masters degrees so they could bounce ideas off each other and that was very helpful. Several colleagues, including the tutor of the control group, were ready to sit down and talk about the research and what he needed to look out for. Not all researchers are so fortunate.

We asked him whether he had experienced any real problems during the course of his research. He said that it took a lot of his time but most of it was fairly straightforward. He had no real problems with the quantitative part of the research but he wasn't comfortable in his role as interviewer. When he started, he didn't have the technique needed to be able to look at qualitative data. He accumulated a lot of data but found difficulty in analysing it. He's learnt more about it now, but at the time it made him uneasy. That wasn't his only area of anxiety:

> One of the things that gave me some trouble was the assumption I made at the start. For example, I assumed the students would tell me everything honestly and openly but when I saw the data, I realized there was a strong bias there. I should have realized that because I was the teacher, some of them were bound to say 'Yes' if that was the response they thought I wanted. I didn't address these assumptions before I began the interviews and that freaked me out quite a bit and I couldn't see how I was going to deal with the bias. I shan't make that mistake again.

You will have gathered that Cher Ping was not what might be described as an average student. He was very focused, appeared to need no more than five hours' sleep a night, worked until 3.00 a.m. if necessary and tried never to lose the impetus of the study, even if he could only manage a couple of hours of reading and writing a day. Few of us can keep up such a regime for ever – or even for a short time! He took the full three years allowed for part-time MEd research studies and it was hard work, but, looking back, he considered the experience was good for him. It stood him in good stead when he started a full-time PhD in England, which he completed in just two years. Now he's on the staff of the National Institute of Education in Singapore and is still continuing with his research.

Could he have got more out of his data? Yes, he probably could if he had been working towards a PhD. The preparation was certainly good enough to have enabled the research to develop up to doctoral standard but he was working towards a MEd and what he did was more than sufficient. And sometimes, researchers need a strong tutor or a good friend who will say 'Stop. No more reading. No more going back to the field to collect more data. No more agonizing. ENOUGH.'

FURTHER READING

Experimental design
Cohen, L., Manion, L. and Morrison, J. (2000) *Research Methods in Education*, 5th edn. London: Routledge Falmer.
   Chapter 12, pp. 211–25, provides a useful discussion of experimental research.
Greene, J. and D'Oliveira, M. (1982) *Learning to Use Statistical Tests in Psychology*. Buckingham: Open University Press.
   Chapter 2, pp. 12–26, discusses experimental designs with one, two or more independent variables, related and unrelated designs and levels of measurement.
Sapsford, R. and Jupp, V. (1996) *Data Collection and Analysis*. London: Sage.
   Pages 12–20 give a shorter but equally useful insight to the problems of undertaking experimental research.

The mean, median and mode
Cohen, K. and Holliday, M. (1996) *Practical Statistics for Students*. London: Paul Chapman.
   Chapter 5, pp. 22–6, provides an easy-to-read overview of the mean, median and mode. Information about how the mean is calculated when the middle score occurs more than once requires a little more effort.
Goulding, S. (1987) in J. Bell *Doing Your Research Project*. Milton Keynes: Open University Press.

Pages 117–21 provide very good explanations of the differences between the mean, median and mode.

Degrees of freedom

Hinton, P.R. (1996) *Statistics Explained: A Guide for Social Science Students*. London: Routledge.

Pages 50–2 provide one of the clearer explanations of degrees of freedom.

Rose, D. and Sullivan, O. (1996) *Introducing Data Analysis for Social Scientists*, 2nd edn. Buckingham: Open University Press.

Chapter 9, pp. 164–78, is quite a hard read but worth the effort. It deals with probability distribution, tests of significance, estimating the *t*-distribution and comparison of sample means. Page 172 provides an example of the table of critical values of *t*.

Hypothesis testing

Greene, J. and D'Oliveira, M. (1982) *Learning to Use Statistical Tests in Psychology*. Buckingham: Open University Press.

Pages 7–8 provide a brief but clear explanation of experimental hypothesis testing.

Pages 35–40 cover selecting statistical tests, looking up probabilities in statistical tables and degrees of freedom.

Rose, D. and Sullivan, O. (1996) *Introducing Data Analysis for Social Scientists*, 2nd edn. Buckingham: Open University Press.

Pages 168–9 discuss the function of the null hypothesis.

t-tests

Clarke, G.M. and Cooke, D. (1992) *A Basic Course in Statistics*, 3rd edn. London: Edward Arnold.

Chapter 16, pp. 251–76, 'Significance tests using the normal distribution', is useful, though quite dense. Pages 265–70 consider t-tests.

Cramer, D. (1997) *Basic Statistics for Social Research*. London: Routledge.

Pages 67–111 discuss statistical significance and probability.

Denscombe, M. (1998) *The Good Research Guide*. Buckingham: Open University Press.

Pages 201–4 provide a brief but clear discussion of t-tests, but the whole of Chapter 10, 'Quantitative Data' (pp. 177–206) is worth reading. It covers types of quantitative data; preparing quantitative data for analysis; presentation of data; discussion of basic statistics; tests of association and difference; and disadvantages of quantitative analysis.

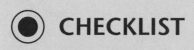

CHECKLIST

1 Read as much as you can before you begin to refine your ideas and decide finally on the focus of your topic.	Don't be in too much of a hurry to finalize your research topic. As you read, themes begin to emerge. Make a note of what you read as you go along.
2 Your research findings may not result in a giant leap forward for education.	But they may well be of relevance to others and therefore of value.
3 Make sure you obtain official permission to carry out your research.	The last thing you need is to find you are refused access to materials and people once your research is underway.
4 Take great care to ensure you are aware of institutional and professional ethical guidelines and the dilemmas of experimental research.	Be careful about promising anonymity and confidentiality.
5 In an experimental study, you will need to establish a control and an experimental group.	Every effort should be made to make groups identical or, if that's not possible, as similar as possible.
6 If you plan to use commercial, externally produced software, make sure you have enough time to familiarize yourself with it and to adapt it for your own and your students' requirements.	AND, make sure the budget for purchase of the software has been agreed. Sounds obvious but . . .

7 Devise hypotheses which will serve as the basis of your research.	Wording has to be precise because not only do hypotheses predict the relationship between sets of data but they also indicate the data needed for the testing to take place.
8 Produce a plan for data collection and analysis.	This will not only make it clear to readers what you plan to do. It will also help you to be quite clear what you can reasonably do in the time – and what you can't.
9 Look for and take advice about which statistical applications are appropriate for your purposes.	Make sure you understand the rationale for the selection of tests and how to apply them.
10 If you're planning interviews and/or observations, prepare schedules and/or check lists and try them out. They always need piloting, no matter how short of time you are.	Be precise about what you need to know. You will only have a limited time to interview or observe and you need to get as much out of the time as you can. Consider what is relevant to your investigation and what is likely to be a waste of time.
11 Always acknowledge the limitations of your study.	It's unlikely you'll be able to claim there are none. Correction. You'll never be able to say there are none!

12 Try to remember that writing always takes much longer than you think. Allow a reasonable amount of time and double it. Then add a bit more and you'll probably be about right. And then just a bit more in case you run into difficulties or there's a crisis at work or at home.

If ever you say 'Right. Nearly finished. I've collected all the data and all I've got to do now is write it up and sort out the references', you're in trouble. Write up as much as you can as you go along. Keep your notes in the sort of good order which ensures you will be able to find and understand them and *never* think 'it's nearly finished' if you've left all the writing to the end, because it won't be.

● Part 4

THE ETHNOGRAPHIC STUDY

Purpose of the study ● refining the topic ● the research focus ● boundaries ● ethnography ● ethnographic methods and techniques ● analysis of documentary data ● the importance of precise definition of terminology ● reading, noting and collating source material ● review of the literature ● the research contract ● the principle of informed consent ● methods of data collection ● the fieldwork ● the interviews ● the stakeholders ● the gatekeepers ● triangulation ● personal involvement ● the development of skills and understanding ● management of information ● in and out of the fog ● analysis of the data ● findings ● reflection ● discussion.

4.1

STATEMENT OF THE PROBLEM and PURPOSE OF THE STUDY

The first doctoral study to be considered here is a Doctor of Philosophy (PhD) thesis produced by Jan Gray (Gray 2000). Jan had been awarded a prestigious university prize for the research she did in connection with her MEd degree and subsequently she was awarded a scholarship which funded her for the necessary three years of full-time doctoral research at a Western Australian university. Before and during her MEd programme, she had been a teacher in various secondary schools in Australia, had become keenly interested in patterns of school non-attendance and behaviour and thought she might wish to select school non-attendance as her PhD topic.

She knew from her teaching and life experience that if teenagers don't want to go to school, they won't go and no amount of legislation will make them go. However, compulsory education is the internationally accepted indicator of commitment to the rights of the child and in most Western countries, including Jan's home territory of Western Australia, that commitment is linked to a legal framework designed to enforce school attendance. A new Western Australian Education Bill was being developed at the time she first began to consider how she might plan her research. The Bill followed the usual pattern of defining truancy, and then establishing a legal framework which she described as being 'on the punitive hierarchical scale moving from fines to detention for degrees of non-compliance'. Several years of consultation and discussion of issues followed and was only enacted towards the end of Jan's period of research.

She was particularly anxious to discover which factors influenced, or might have influenced, popular beliefs about truancy and which contributed to the creation and enactment of public policy. In other words, she wanted to be able to 'read' the culture of compulsory education and decision-making processes. This was quite a task, not to be undertaken without considerable time and thought being spent on focusing the topic. She recalls:

> At that time, I was thinking in terms of non-attendance but it was too broad a research area and so I narrowed it down to truancy. I didn't think of it in terms of compulsory attendance, but in terms of why students who didn't want to be at school were compelled to attend. My sense was that inevitably it (that is compulsory attendance) wasn't going to work. I wanted to know what made people believe that it would work when it never had before. That's where I started.

She had no illusions about the difficulties she would face in carrying out an investigation of this kind:

> I knew I was going to have as much trouble in writing the theoretical framing of the topic as in articulating how I was going to carry out this project, step by step. It was a twofold thing, how to describe that theoretical sense of development of knowledge and to understand why people framed and implemented policy in a certain way – as well as being an illustration of truancy.

The research focus

Jan's research focused on the social definition of a 'truant' and on the cultural factors which influenced beliefs about truancy. She needed to understand why people felt and believed the way they did; why policemen on truancy patrols believed so strongly that what they were told to do, such as returning absentee children to school, was right. Was it possible that the perceived incidence of truancy within a community had more impact on the creation and enactment of public policy than the incidence itself? Questions, questions, questions, each one of which produced yet more questions. She knew she had to start somewhere and in order to progress the planning, she devised three fundamental though very broad questions which she anticipated would provide the framework for her research. They were:

- In what ways has a particular view of truancy produced specific perceptions and responses to youth and compulsory education?
- What cultural factors have influenced popular and academic beliefs about truancy?
- In what ways have these responses influenced the creation and enactment of public policy associated with truancy?

The context and boundaries of the topic

She had three years as a full-time researcher but that was little enough time to get to grips with the complexities of the topic. The more she thought about what would be involved, the clearer it became that an individual case study of a school or even of one education district would be unlikely to give her the necessary insight and understanding. She needed breadth and that meant she would need access to educational and judicial institutions across several school districts in order to become part of the decision-making processes within institutions. Four education districts were finally included in the investigation, one of which was selected for detailed study. And so the investigation became bigger and bigger. It became apparent that this was to be an ethnographic study which required immersion in the culture of compulsory education.

We asked Jan what she understood by **ethnography**. She described it as

a search for meaning, the reading of a culture, the development of an understanding of how a culture works, whether

it's of an institution, a classroom or the culture of a phenomenon, which was what I was attempting.

In order to achieve such understanding, she made use of many
ethnographic methods and techniques which, as Lutz points out,
include, though are not limited to

> participant observation, interview, mapping and charting,
> interaction analysis, study of historical records and current
> public documents, use of demographic data, etc. But ethno-
> graphy centers on the participant observation of a society or
> culture through a complete cycle of events that regularly
> occur as that society interacts with its environment . . .

It also centres on the

> interactive processes involving the discovery of important
> and recurring variables in the society as they relate to one
> another, under specified conditions, and as they affect or
> produce certain results and outcomes in the society.
> (Lutz 1986: 108)

The question for us is *how* did Jan set out to identify these
important and recurring variables in the society she was researching? *What* methods and techniques did she use? *What* worked
well during the course of the research and what didn't? And did
her search for meaning finally enable her to 'read' the elusive
culture of compulsory education in her selected geographical
areas?

The following pages present her account of ethnography in
practice, the fieldwork she carried out over the period of her
research, the tasks she undertook, what she learnt about her
topic and about *ethnographic research*. But before she could
begin, she needed to inform herself about truancy legislation in
her research area and elsewhere.

4.2

SETTING THE SCENE and the ANALYSIS OF DOCUMENTARY EVIDENCE

Jan knew that before she could consider planning her methods of data collection, she had to inform herself about truancy legislation in Western Australia and to examine the reports of research already carried out on her topic in Australia and in other Western countries. She began with an examination of previous Western Australian Education Acts, reports and other documentation in the public domain and this source material provided detailed background information about the way truancy legislation had (or had not) developed over the years.

Her reading was very thorough and very detailed and the following summary of the Western Australian 'official' documentation gives some idea of the lengths to which she went to obtain the necessary information that allowed her to start her research from an informed base.

She started with a study of definitions of truancy in the Western Australian context.

The Western Australian Education Acts

The first step was to consult Western Australian Education Acts from 1928 onwards which included definitions (though no common, agreed definition) of school truancy on the lines of 'the persistent, habitual and unexplained absence from school of a child of compulsory school age' and 'a child who is absent from school without an acceptable reason is considered to be committing the offence of truancy and the parent is liable to prosecution'. Interpretation of truancy covered such items as number of days or points in the day, truancy with or without parental knowledge and consent, numbers of days' suspension permitted at any one time, responsibilities of parents, and so on.

The 1999 School Education Bill and the subsequent Act abandoned the term 'truancy' and replaced it with 'absentee student'. As far as Jan could see, the change of terminology made no significant difference to the implied reliance on judicial intervention to enforce school attendance, though a number of changes in structure were introduced. The establishment of School Attendance Panels (SAPs) was proposed in order to allow opportunities for what was hoped to be successful intervention in cases of absentee students; the locus of responsibility was to be shifted to the local school, allowing the School Welfare Officer (SWO) to take an advisory role and to concentrate on 'chronic' cases.

It was important for her to understand the legal position relating to truancy as specified in the Bill and the subsequent Act and the range of responsibilities of the newly established panels, committees and individual officers, as she hoped to be given permission to participate in panel and committee meetings, to interview members of the panels and of the SWOs.

Reports and other documentation

After the Education Acts, Jan moved on to examine the very large number of reports and other documentation relating to truancy which were in the public domain and which were produced by the Education Department of Western Australia (EDWA) and other agencies. The search for documentary data was not all plain sailing. It rarely is. She discovered that some data were available only to individual schools, their SWOs, related student service personnel and district directors. She was concerned that some of these data might be crucial to her understanding of the extent and nature of truancy in her selected districts, but truancy was a sensitive issue and not all schools were anxious to have such data made public. There was particular secrecy about any data indicating levels of suspension and exclusion within school districts. That was hardly surprising in view of the fact that when such data were obtained by the media through Freedom of Information legislation, publication triggered a series of moral panics and front page coverage in newspapers. Even so, some newspaper databases provided valuable sources of information and gave insight into the interaction between media images, public perceptions and belief systems within a community and what she saw as media-instigated panics about the extent of truancy in the districts she was investigating.

The analysis of documentary evidence did not end once the preliminary stage of reading had finished. It was ongoing through-out the research. As she became known to and trusted by particip-ants, more and more documentary data were made available to her but in the beginning she had to make do with what was available for public scrutiny. She had no choice but to bide her time, build up trust and hope that eventually her participants would feel sufficiently comfortable with her to make confiden-tial documents available for scrutiny. She was not able to use documents which she knew to be confidential but many of the databases she examined offered rich sources of information which contributed to her understanding of some of the key issues. She was given sight of sensitive items such as suspension databases and, in one year, read 3185 incident reports which had been forwarded by schools to district offices, all valuable data which would never have been made available at the start of the re-search. And in case it begins to read as though truancy was a massive problem in the four education districts included in this research, we should probably mention that truancy was at the time running at around 4 per cent (based on the legal definition of 'truancy') compared with what was reported as the more usual 10 per cent in the USA and UK research literature. Having said that, Jan was as aware as anyone that percentages of this kind mean little unless the definition of truancy is consistently known and applied. She recalls that in one school meeting she asked for their truancy statistics which seemed to her to be surprisingly high. She then asked for the school's definition of truancy which produced a variety of responses. Once a common definition was applied it appeared the truancy rate had miraculously halved! It may have been all right for Humpty Dumpty to say that 'it (whatever "it" refers to) means just what I choose it to mean – neither more nor less', but lack of precision in meaning and definition among members of panels, committees *and* researchers can result in critical misunderstandings and errors of judgement. Imprecision is serious.

4.3

THE REVIEW OF THE LITERATURE

As can be imagined, the amount of information Jan obtained from official and semi-official documents was very large, and the extent of the published research into issues relating to truancy was equally large. She was not new to research when she began her PhD. She knew she had to produce a review of the literature and she also knew that producing a review from the large amount of literature she absorbed not only at the start but also throughout the period of the research was likely to be taxing. Because of her experience she could guess at some likely themes but she was always on the lookout for new or unexpected topics. It's fairly easy to produce what Haywood and Wragg, perhaps rather unkindly, describe as the furniture sale catalogue

in which everything merits a one-paragraph entry no matter how skilfully it has been conducted: Bloggs (1975) found this, Smith (1976) found that, Jones (1977) found the other, Bloggs, Smith and Jones (1978) found happiness in heaven.
(Haywood and Wragg 1982: 2)

It's quite another matter to provide a *critical* review of the literature which demonstrates 'that the writer has studied existing work in the field with insight' (Haywood and Wragg 1982: 2) and which 'should provide the reader with a picture . . . of the state of knowledge and of major questions in the subject being investigated' (Bell 1999: 93). This was the challenge facing Jan and which faces all other researchers who have reached the stage of producing a logical and coherent account of the current state of knowledge in their field.

Do you recall Cher Ping's description of how he managed his reading and his review of the literature in Part 3? He made it sound easy but it isn't. It requires his degree of discipline in always being on the lookout for themes, groupings, patterns and possible key issues. It involves ensuring that every single source is fully referenced and in having the insight to move items from one thematic group to another when the emphasis changes, as it probably will as the research progresses. It requires sifting, selecting and ordering of material, including only important items and ruthlessly rejecting irrelevant or less significant items. And that's hard.

Clara Nai, a very successful Masters student, recalled her dismay at discovering that she had to reject most of what she had read when she was preparing her review. At the time, she considered it was 'so unfair that only a fraction of the months of painstaking reading could appear in print' (Nai 1996: 33). What she read provided her with essential background information about many aspects of her research topic but, as always happens, she had to filter the mass of information obtained from her reading for inclusion in her review of the literature.

All researchers try to conduct the main part of their literature review in the early days of the investigation but, inevitably over a three-year period, new research reports appear, different perceptions emerge and it becomes necessary to return to the literature. The documentary analysis Jan carried out throughout the three years of the research enabled her to have an understanding of local and international perceptions of truancy. As happens with all large-scale reviews of the literature, she was able to identify recurring themes which she eventually decided to categorize under the headings of Legal Construction, Academic Construction, Community Construction and Historical Construction. Her review was very detailed and we do not have the space to include all of it, but the following extracts and summaries give some idea of the way she approached this particular task.

Legal construction

In Chapter 2, we considered some of the Education Acts, reports and other documentation made available to Jan before her data collecting began and throughout the time of the research. In her review, she highlights key issues in the legal frameworks in place in most Western countries 'in which non-compliance with such directives is defined as truancy and has become an internationally accepted part of the culture of schooling'. She discusses the implications of the numerous definitions of truancy, intervention strategies and school disciplinary practice. Referring particularly to practice in Western Australia, she concludes this part of her review by saying that, from the evidence of her reading, it appeared that

> the legal construction of school non-attendance centred on a belief . . . in the power of punishment as an effective deterrent for both non-compliant students and their parents. This hierarchy of deterrence factors is reflected in the regulatory framework underpinning school behaviour management policies, incorporating isolation, suspension and exclusion of non-compliant students.

Academic construction

The 'Academic construction' section concentrates on numerous studies which claimed to have discovered an amazing range of factors contributing to or causing truancy. One of the most bizarre claimed a high correlation between truancy and masturbation (reported in Cashen's 1992 study of compulsory education in South Australia between 1927 and 1930)! However, as we pointed out in Gilbert's section on *correlation* and *causation* (pp. 66–7), just because two variables have a high positive correlation doesn't necessarily mean that one is the cause of the other.

Various studies identified vulnerability triggers such as antisocial attitudes prevalent in working-class communities; gender and age; neurotic disorders indicative of disturbed family relationships; effects of labelling on both teachers' and students' perceptions of truancy; stress; low school achievement and motivation; and exposure to drug usage. Other international and Australian research identified risk factors for those leaving school before the legal age which included homelessness; illiteracy; low socio-economic status; abuse (as perpetrator and/or victim); dysfunctional family background; academic failure; substance abuse; and physical, social and intellectual disability. All these factors may well have an impact on truancy but, as Jan points out, 'the wide range of definitions used in studies of intermittent truancy constantly confounds any projections of degree, correlation of contributing factors and seriousness of the truancy problem'.

Community construction

In this section, Jan identifies issues raised in statistical surveys, published research, media and conference reports. She discusses assumptions within communities, such as the rights of elders to control and mould the behaviour of their youth and the assumed link between youth and crime. She studied crime statistics, reports on research into the influence of the media and concludes that 'information regarding truancy patterns, causes, proactive and reactive responses to truancy constitute the working assumptions of journalists and policy makers who write about, speak about, or create policy related to containment of the problem'.

She gives particular emphasis in this section to research carried out into what she describes as 'the concept of moral panic as a form of social control' and concludes that 'the power of the image constantly presented to the public, confirmed by self-perpetuating research, is significant'. She summarizes her findings by saying that

> counter to the promoted image of the youth/crime nexus, recent local and international evidence [sources provided by Jan] questions the assumed and reported dramatic increases in crime associated with youth and demonstrates no per capita rise in crime rate. In fact, the overwhelming evidence

shows most young offenders commit one, maybe two relatively minor offences, usually whilst drug and peer group affected, then return to the societal fold. Although there is a small proportion of young repeat offenders, members of the youth age group are the most likely *victims* of petty and violent crime.

Historical construction

The 'Historical construction' section follows the path through the establishment of compulsory education from its introduction in Western Australia in 1899 'as a response to an identified societal need'. In her reading and rereading of the establishment and development of compulsory education, she identifies several conflicting paradigms, one based on the benign view that people should be educated for the common and for their own good. What she describes as the other, revisionist, explanation utilized 'a Marxist concept of the state as the embodiment of bourgeois power and economic self-interest'. Over the years, there were many fingers in the compulsory education pie, including the involvement of churches which played a significant role 'as a means of containment of children supposedly roaming the streets, making nuisances of themselves'.

In the first two decades of the twentieth century, there was recognition of the increasing presence of a young, street population 'reflecting the changing demographics of a new colony, and whose visibility on the streets was irritating to the authorities'. The term 'delinquent' came into being and many changes to enforcement and punishment structures were justified as part of the move to deterrence, as were changes in the direction of the law from catching and punishing the unruly child to identifying a particular type of child in order to treat the condition of delinquency. At one stage, parental unwillingness to send children to school was believed to indicate neglect, indifference and truancy, all of which were seen to be a warning of future emotional problems, maladjustment and 'pre-delinquency tendencies' whereas in the 1950s, creation of delinquents was believed to be caused by parental over-indulgence. And so the 'reasons for' and 'causes of' delinquency and truancy continued to have an airing until the present day, which led Jan to conclude:

> A common community construction of today's student reflects nostalgic notions of innocence and family values, manifested as a fear of loss of control. The student who rejects school is seen by the community to be undermining ideals, a threat to social order. For an adult community, especially for adult educators and law enforcement agencies, the 'schooled child' is by far a more comforting construction than the 'delinquent child'.

* * *

Drawing together the threads

This extensive review highlights the major implications of issues discussed in each of the four constructions and draws particular attention to what Jan describes as the 'complex interrelationship between these diverse constructions'. When she moved into the fieldwork stage of her research, she began to understand just how complex those interrelationships were – but more of that later.

Before the data collecting began, and throughout the review, she drew on a wide and varied range of well-referenced international and national research and on her intensive study of Education Acts and other documentation. That enabled her to discriminate between the way beliefs about truancy developed and the well-documented and authenticated reality of the situation. Without that background, she would have begun the process of interviewing, observing and participating from an uninformed standpoint which would not only have been damaging to her credibility but would also have limited the usefulness of her data collecting.

We've given more space to Jan's review of the literature than in any of the other reviews discussed so far in this book but even so, we have only had the space to provide extracts from and summaries of large sections. Inevitably, we've left out a great deal more than we have included but as far as you can judge from this limited selection, did she seem to have provided a balanced account of the published research and the documentary data she discusses? Were there signs of *bias* (that is selecting only those items which supported her point of view) or use of inappropriate language? Again, as far as you are able to judge, is there evidence that she had 'studied existing work in the field with insight' (Haywood and Wragg 1982: 2)? Finally, did her review overall provide you 'with a picture . . . of the state of knowledge and of major questions in the subject being investigated' (Bell 1999: 93)?

4.4

THE RESEARCH CONTRACT
AND THE PRINCIPLE OF
INFORMED CONSENT

Permission for the research to be carried out was, of course, obtained before the documentary study began, but Jan felt, quite rightly, that she should make absolutely sure that she and the likely stakeholders interpreted the wording of the originally agreed conditions of research in the same way. As we keep saying, words can mean different things to different people and there was no room for any later and unanticipated hitches which might have jeopardized the investigation. It's always as well to be absolutely sure that permission given in principle holds good in practice.

Many ethnographers (and other qualitative *and* quantitative researchers, come to that) stress the importance of establishing some sort of 'contract' with the research participants and organizations to be studied, and this is sound practice – from the point of view of all concerned. Lutz specifies what, in his opinion, should always be agreed beforehand.

Such a 'contract' may include specifications about what records may and may not be examined; where the ethnographer may or may not go, when, and under what circumstances; which meetings may be attended and which are closed; how long the researcher will stay in the field; who (if anyone) has access to the field notes, and even who has the right to review and/or approve the ethnography and its analysis prior to publication, or under what circumstances they may or may not be published at all.

(Lutz 1986: 114)

We fully agree with this approach. Jan was moving into sensitive areas and knew she had to take great care to ensure that participants understood their and her own role in the research. She was determined that none of her participants or organizations would in any way be damaged as a result of the research, that confidentiality would never be threatened and no individual would be identified in her thesis (see Sapsford and Abbott 1996: 318–22). She knew that a large part of her data would come from interviews and so she decided that wherever possible she would obtain the 'informed consent' of participants beforehand. The procedures she adopted were as follows:

- Before interviews began, she introduced herself as a researcher, gave information about the nature of the research, guaranteed confidentiality and anonymity (and explained what each meant), made clear who would have sight or knowledge of her findings and ensured that permission had been given for audio-recording.
- Where appropriate, participants were sent a consent letter and in some cases were invited to sign a consent form. The letters varied according to the role and background of participants.
- Key participants were promised an interview transcript and, if necessary, the opportunity to discuss, negotiate and collaboratively refine content and wording.

Not surprisingly, she ran into some difficulties over the time involved in transcribing interviews. Though she could not in any way depart from the university's ethics rules, she knew she would not have the time to provide full interview transcripts and so she had to amend the wording of her contract. In the early cases of the delayed interview transcripts, she contacted the interviewees and said something on the lines of:

Sorry for the delay but would it be OK if I just sent you a copy of the points I think I might wish to use in the thesis?

I've left out all our conversation bits. If you would like the whole thing, I'll get it transcribed or I can send you a copy of the tape. Just let me know. If I don't hear from you by (a certain date), I'll assume the shortened transcript is acceptable to you and that you have no queries.

And they all accepted that. The process of forwarding interview transcripts to interviewees and then negotiating and refining the wording and content could have presented problems because of the time involved. As it happened, only one person asked for clarification of a few points and they were quickly dealt with.

Not everything went according to plan and obtaining informed consent very occasionally became the barrier beyond which a few participants simply would not enter the study but in general the principle worked well, ensured there were no misunderstandings and provided a firm basis for the fieldwork stage of the research.

4.5

THE FIELDWORK

There was no way of recognizing who were the image makers and identifying what Jan described as 'the framing influences within a culture' other than by becoming immersed in the daily workings of the related cultures of educational, police and juvenile justice district offices. Knowing and understanding the territory and, above all, establishing trust can't be achieved by carrying out a few interviews and dropping in at a few meetings.

It was probably inevitable that the original time allocated for data collection had to be extended in order to accommodate the whole gamut of policy processes associated with school non-attendance. In fact, she found she frequently had to return to the field beyond the initial data-collecting period, which can be dangerous. Such a practice has been known to result in the researcher collecting more and more data but never quite managing to get down to the task of deciding what to do with it.

One legitimate reason for her regular return to the field was that her original neat time line did not always coincide with real life. She wished to follow the progress of some students from their first reported truancy to their final exclusion from school, but the dates for exclusion and review panels and appearances in court were not fixed for Jan's convenience. They occurred throughout the year and she just had to fit in with those arrangements.

Methods of data collection

Many different methods of data collection were used, including participant and non-participant observation; formal and informal interviewing of key participants within each district; interaction with and observation of key individuals in their work environment; sharing stories; shadowing professionals during the course of their work (and helping them to gather and collate their data); attending meetings; and listening to and participating in conversations. Inevitably, one method merged into another.

She acted as participant observer to selection panels for alternative education programmes and many formal and informal meetings; interviewed senior personnel from four local shires, district directors of the education departments, the justice department, the police and other related agencies. She chaired 12 exclusion panels, actively participated in attendance panels for seven chronic truants and attended four inter-agency meetings involving the police. Meetings and panels proved to be a major focus of the data collection because they were the forum in which policy was created and enacted.

She recalls that it was the constant questioning of practice and *reflexivity* which provided the basis of an understanding of the culture and context appropriate to each element of the spectrum. Brewer reminds us that reflexivity

> involves reflection by ethnographers on the social processes that impinge upon and influence data. It requires a critical attitude towards data, and recognition of the influence on the research of such factors as the location of the setting, the sensitivity of the topic and the nature of the social interaction between the researcher and the researched.
>
> (Brewer 2000: 191)

We shall return to the principle of reflexivity later, but for the time being we'll consider the role of key participants in the study and what Jan discovered from them about their practice and beliefs.

Key individuals, groups, institutions and agencies (the stakeholders)

One day a week for six months was spent shadowing one of the SWOs in order to develop an appreciation and understanding of the SWO role and to establish contact with various other stakeholders. Jan participated on home visits, at inter-agency meetings and panels and had lengthy interviews with other SWOs.

This pattern of observation, two-hour taped interviews, informal untaped interviews and committee and panel membership was continued with many other stakeholders such as youth legal advisers, Juvenile Justice Education Officers, youth workers, social workers in the Education Department, Aboriginal Welfare Officers, staff of Family and Children's Services, school principals and teachers, parents of truants and with the truants themselves. Interaction with the police was never formalized into taped interviews, but she was allowed to shadow staff assigned to truancy patrols and to observe the work of the police in district police stations.

The interviews

Regardless of whether interviews were formal or informal, taped or not taped, Jan asked questions on the lines of 'What do you do?' followed by 'How do you do it? How do you work with these students? What leeway do you have in dealing with them? Who do you work with in other institutions?' She couldn't begin to understand *why* they did things in certain ways until she had figured out *what* they were doing. She had to be able to understand what people saw as their role and their context, to ask them why they did things in one way rather than another and to understand why they thought the way they were doing things was appropriate. It was not always easy for interviewees to answer the 'why' questions and when Jan looked some time later at the transcripts and listened again to the tapes it became clear that as the discussions developed, the people concerned were in the process of constructing and reconstructing their role. It was like a training process and it reached the point where in some cases she felt she understood their role better than they did. Over time, she moved up in her level of thinking about how everything fitted together, but it certainly took a long time.

Gatekeepers

She very particularly wished to establish contact with alienated youth, particularly students who were classified as chronic truants, whose life experiences provoked an active reluctance to sign any 'official' form or to be subjected to any authority figure. She was an outsider and she knew she would not obtain access unless she was accompanied by a 'gatekeeper' who was someone they knew and trusted. Two school principals and one SWO took on the role of chief gatekeepers. It often took what she described as 'layers of gatekeeping' before parental permission was given. Access had to be negotiated, conditions agreed and assurances given about confidentiality and often it depended on the gate-keeper saying 'She's OK. You can talk in front of her. She won't tell anybody anything you say unless you agree.' Once trust was established and it became clear that she had no judgemental agenda, discussion became open and informative. Several Aboriginal parents eventually became active participants in the study and agreed that interviews could be taped. Students began to volunteer comments and opinions, none of which were 'official'. She found their comments vital to the study and integrated them throughout the body of the work as third person alienated youth perspectives, though in ways which ensured they could not be traced to a particular location or student.

One point of concern was that she was not sure if all the Aboriginal interviewees would be literate and so she had to allow sufficient time for them to find someone who would help by reading the transcripts and telling them what they said. She was anxious that they might be critical but in fact they were interested to share their stories and their life histories, so all was well.

Personal involvement

She found she was becoming personally involved and, in ethnographic research, involvement is difficult to avoid. She was well aware of what she described as 'my own controlling image in developing an understanding of the cultures underpinning the framing of public policy associated with truancy' and of her potential as a researcher to affect the practice of participants. She discovered there were no safe places from which merely to observe and that as an ethnographic researcher 'it was not possible to avoid the *dialectic* between the observed and the interpreted worlds'. There can be few ethnographic researchers who have not made this uneasy discovery, though the dialectic is or can be an important step in the direction of understanding and representing new knowledge.

The development of skills and understanding

As the research continued, Jan began to develop skills of interacting and observing, as she knew she must. She began to recognize and become sensitive to the image makers; to interpret the interaction within and between agencies and institutions involved with young people who were defined as truants; to recognize the subtle (and often shifting) power relationships during inter-agency meetings and to develop understanding of symbolic meanings and cultural contexts.

The investigation proved to be far more complex than she had at first thought. Though she understood the importance of many of the issues involved in her topic before she began the research, she quickly discovered that she really didn't understand the decision-making processes involved at all. She just had to get in there and start to find out how things were done, when, why and how, and that involved a longer period of data collecting than she had anticipated.

The management of information

We asked how she managed all the information. Her reply was that the first stage was management by box, but with the clear intention of transferring summaries and what she considered to be important items of information into computer files and folders, which is what she did. She even created what she called a 'dump file' so that nothing was actually lost. However, her cardboard boxes continued to exist until she had time to analyse their contents and to create the files. She had a cardboard box for the justice system, one for education, another for police etc., into which she put all their policies and legislative material, together with interview transcripts. Tapes were put into shoe boxes and the good thing about shoe and cardboard boxes is that they look as if everything is well organized and that encourages depressed researchers to believe that the research is in good shape. It also ensures that visitors don't come to the conclusion that you prefer paper to carpet on your floors. In a lengthy period of data collecting, there have to be ways of storing the ever-increasing mountain of paper. The only problem is that experience has shown that, though it's easy to put information neatly into a box or, come to that, a computer file, it can be much harder to devise a system which ensures you'll be able to find it some time later. Useless to say 'I'll remember where I put the field notes on East Grimly School because I've put them at the back of that bright yellow folder with the Mickey Mouse sticker on it.' You won't find them, unless there is some sophisticated system of indexing. The sticker might have fallen off, the file might have been removed – and you just won't remember where those notes are when another hundred sets of field notes have been slotted in. The boxes and files can become the equivalent of black holes into which everything goes but nothing emerges.

We all know that tapes, reports, notes of meetings and transcripts (entire or selective) must be kept in case they are needed for later checking and Jan never threw anything away. She developed a cross-indexing system to ensure she could find what she was looking for and at the time she wanted it. Tiresome, but not nearly as tiresome as having to spend days trying to find some particularly important item which you know must be somewhere in one of those boxes. The system is immaterial as long as it works for you, but if there's no system established from the start, that equals disaster.

Even though Jan was always systematic about the filing and reviewing of data, she reached a stage when the amount of paper she was generating began to overwhelm her and she knew she wasn't coping, particularly with the transcribing of interviews. In other words, she was suffering from that well-known disease called data overload, and data overload leads to problems over data retrieval and analysis. She had acquired what Miles and Huberman (1994: 56) describe as 'an alpine collection of information that might require a week just to read over carefully'. The problem is that in the early days we have little idea what is, or might be, interesting and what is not and so we tend to keep everything.

They argue that the analysis of qualitative data presents particular difficulties because it is done chiefly with words, not with numbers:

> Words are fatter than numbers and usually have multiple meanings. This makes them harder to move around and work with. Worse still, most words are meaningless unless you look backward or forward to other words . . . The second dilemma is embedded in the first; within that mass of data, you may not know – or may not have tagged – the pieces that matter the most for the purposes of your study.
>
> The challenge is to be explicitly mindful of the purpose of your study and of the conceptual lenses you are training on it – while allowing yourself to be open to and reeducated by things you didn't know about or didn't expect to find.
>
> (Miles and Huberman 1994: 56)

They urge researchers to resist overload at the time they are collecting their data, though not at the price of sketchiness. As they admit, that is easier said than done, though they do offer a few suggestions about how it might be achieved:

> To do it, you will need a variety of safeguards against tunnel vision, bias, and self-delusion . . . Just as important, you will

have to accompany each wave of data collection with a corresponding exercise in condensation and analysis (p. 56).

They calculate that it takes between two and five times as much time to process and order data as it took to collect it and if analysis is not to become a nightmare, time has to be allowed for that in the overall allowance for the collection of data. We believe them.

In fact, Jan did her utmost to analyse her data as she transcribed interviews. Her analysis was informed by ongoing reference to the literature and to the emerging themes but it took an enormous amount of time. She thought her original timing took account of the need to process her raw data but the recordings, transcriptions and field notes came in more quickly than she could deal with them. As she had to fit in with her participants' commitments, that sometimes meant she was on the intensive data collection trail for longer periods than she would have wished.

She recalls:

I figured I wasn't going to be able to eat and sleep let alone keep up with the research if I kept on the way I was. I was driving my family nuts and it just wasn't feasible. So, I started getting smart about it. I made sure I kept to what I'd promised in the research contract but only transcribed parts of interviews, panel and other reports so I was actually culling it all as I went along.

It seems to us that the only way to avoid data overload is to do what Jan did – or something like it.

Into and out of the fog

Jan reached a point in the period of data collection when she felt as if she were groping her way in a dense fog and would never be able to find a way out of it. She had a vast amount of information which related to public perceptions of truancy but for a long time she could not see how each item related to the rest. She could not identify the power bases nor the particular belief systems which underpinned the creation and enactment of public policy relating to school non-attendance. There were too many threads, too many individuals with the same job title but who were working in different ways. Too many different views, beliefs and contradictions. She seemed constantly to be identifying new themes, issues and concepts.

She heard many stories and they, together with recordings of meetings and unstructured informal conversations, field notes and impressions gained from transcribing the interviews, enabled her to create narrative versions of what she heard and so became one stage in the analysis. But that was only one stage. She was constantly referring back to the legislative and regulatory frameworks and reports of how conditions were applied. Each time she went to see people or to attend a meeting she began to see how some parts fitted into other parts but she just couldn't see the whole picture. She came to realize that she had to step back from the total immersion which had absorbed so much of her time. No more going back to the safety of data collection. No more 'just five more interviews should be enough'. She already had enough data and had to have time 'to allow participants to become abstractions'. This was an important stage in the process of data analysis. By this time, she knew a great deal about what many participants did, their beliefs about truancy and the way they interpreted their own personal role but she also knew she had some way to go before she could see the full picture.

Looking back, she realizes that the process of enlightenment began during one particular inter-agency meeting where each person present was representing a different agency and where she realized she had interviewed everyone who was there. The individuals obviously knew that she had interviewed them but they did not necessarily know that she had also interviewed everyone else. She recalls:

At that stage, I began to realize that I was getting a hold on what was happening. I could see that I had the great advantage of knowing what each thought, the way they constructed their role in one particular way rather than another; how they defined and acted on their particular construct of truancy and what they believed about the culture of compulsory education. I could begin to categorize viewpoints into clusters. All the bits were coming together. I was at last able to understand that this powerful belief system provided the framework within which roles and expertise were delineated, boundaries defined and interaction within and between individuals and institutions could be identified. In other words, I was able to begin to identify what I considered to be the foundational beliefs for the culture of compulsory education.

She didn't know why the fog began to lift in that particular meeting. She just knew that it did and that she was on the way to putting together all the pieces in order to produce that elusive overall picture.

4.6

ANALYSING THE DATA

Raw data are of little use until they have undergone some form of processing. Interviews have to be transcribed, either fully or in the reduced format Jan adopted; field notes and notes taken at meetings have to be reviewed, put into order and edited; decisions have to be made about what is to stay in and what is to be left out. Jan had strong views about the culture of compulsory education. She had not quite gone native but she was certainly involved and she knew she had to return repeatedly to the data in order to be as sure as she could that she was reporting on the data rather than on her own convictions. Similarly, she knew she must be meticulous about what evidence to include and what to exclude – and that's never easy.

The analysis of ethnographic data may not be an exact science, but in Brewer's opinion, that does not mean that it shouldn't be systematic and rigorous. He writes that

> The first thing to note about analysis is that it is a continuous process. Given that ethnography is best perceived as a process rather than a sequence of discrete stages (like all research), data analysis is simultaneous with data collection . . .

Analysis usually begins when the field notes are read and typed before the next visit to the field, when categories, descriptive units and links between the data appear.

(Brewer 2000: 107)

Not unnaturally, in the early days of the investigation, Jan found it difficult to appreciate the significance of her data. She recorded everything and made a note of possible categories, likely key individuals and groups, but it was only really after the 'enlightenment' that she began to see connections, patterns, themes and relationships between individuals, groups and organizations. We have already discussed the importance of devising a system of indexing and cross-referencing (sometimes called index coding) in order to be able to locate information and sources. Without such a system, early and ongoing analysis is impossible.

There were times in her overload period when she was not always able to keep up to the routine of what Miles and Huberman (1994: 10–11) describe as 'data reduction', by which they meant 'the process of selecting, focusing, simplifying, abstracting, and transforming the data that appear in written-up field notes or transcriptions'.

We would agree with Wolcott (1990) that it's not possible to begin writing too early and Jan certainly produced rough-and-ready summaries as they came in. At first it was difficult to understand what was of significance and what was not, but as the data collecting went on it began to make sense to her and possible key categories and themes began to emerge. If her recording and early writing had not been done, she would have been faced with the impossible task of having to face that 'alpine collection of information' (Miles and Huberman 1994: 56) and with little idea about where to start. As it was, the task of analysis, presentation and verification was demanding and the thesis took many drafts before she was satisfied she had presented the evidence as fully and accurately as she possibly could.

The findings

We have not been able to do more than touch on the extent of the data collecting, the number of interviews, committees and panels attended, the talking, listening, shadowing and depth of understanding achieved. Jan recalls that the entire study was a process of learning, discovering, adapting, adjusting boundaries, interpreting, looking for meaning. So what did she discover during that voyage of discovery? Well, quite a lot.

As the research proceeded, she discovered more, read more and eventually was able to summarize her findings in the form of graphs, charts and words. Her reading of confidential reports and surveys provided her with statistics which sometimes conflicted with the official versions. Somehow or another, she had to find ways of verifying one or the other. Clearly both could not be right. She had to test for what Miles and Huberman describe as 'their plausibility, their sturdiness, their "confirm ability" – that is, their *validity*. Otherwise we are left with interesting stories about what happened, of unknown truth and utility' (Miles and Huberman 1994: 11).

Triangulation

She did this by means of triangulation, defined by Cohen and Manion (1994: 233) as 'the use of two or more methods of data collection in the study of some aspect of human behaviour'; by recording and comparing statements and opinions in meetings and in interviews with district education officers, SWOs, lawyers, juvenile justice workers, student services personnel, family and children's services, the police, school staff, community representatives, parents and the non-attenders themselves. She tested specialist databases such as those devised by SWOs against 'official' versions, returning constantly to the data in order to ensure that, as far as was possible, her final version was 'accurate' and to make sure she could not be accused of bias or tunnel vision. She regularly referred back to the literature in order to check the extent to which her findings were the same as or similar to those of other researchers. These steps were necessary or her accounts could have been accused of being little more than an exercise in confirming her own prejudices.

'Reading' the culture of compulsory education

Jan's main purpose in carrying out this investigation was to be able to read the culture of compulsory education and to identify which cultural perspectives had the greatest influence on the development and enactment of laws designed to enforce school attendance – laws which reflected community beliefs in the need for punitive measures. When she began to emerge from the fog and to see where each aspect fitted into the whole, she was able to identify three predominant influences on the framing of public policy associated with truancy, which were:

- the foundational beliefs of a culture;
- the controlling images perpetuated through media, research, textual and cultural representation of truancy; and
- public perceptions of truants and actions portrayed as typical of truancy and perceived as being different by the framing body.

She devised the following figure to illustrate the impact of these influences on public policy.

She found the predominant influences on the development of public policy associated with truancy could be described in terms of three powerful and defining cultures:

> Each one of these cultures reflected the belief in the role of the law as a form of defining, regulating and arbitrating cultural boundaries associated with young people, manifested in powerful and public images and perceptions of truancy.

From her extensive study of the culture of compulsory education, she identified the influences on creating, evoking and enacting public policy on truancy to be *the punitive culture, the culture of dependence and the culture of difference* (see Figure 3).

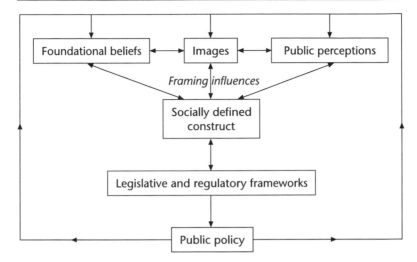

Figure 2 Framing influences for the creation of public policy associated with a socially defined construct
Source: Gray 2000

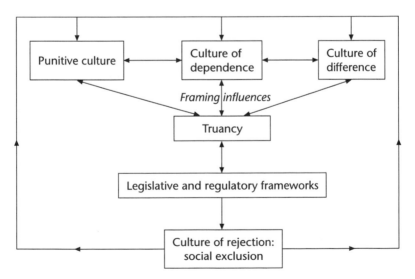

Figure 3 Current framing of public policy associated with non-attendance
Source: Gray 2000

The *punitive culture* was based on 'belief in the institutional power of deterrence and the role of punishment in managing young people's behaviour'. *The culture of dependence* was based on perceived boundaries of ownership of a problem and thus responsibility for providing a solution, and *the culture of difference* was based on a perception of difference indicating potential deviance.

This very brief summary of the influence of the three cultures, once again, does not do justice to the extensive arguments and evidence Jan presented to support her understanding of the impact of these cultures on the legislative and regulatory frameworks which, she concludes, leads to the culture of rejection and social exclusion.

Jan had difficulty in isolating the individual impact of each of these three cultures because of their interrelationship within and belief in each other. Once again she returned to the data, the field notes, the reduced interview transcripts, the recordings, the abstractions and the literature. She checked and rechecked her evidence base and finally drew up lists of ways in which the three cultures impacted, or might have impacted on the enactment of the public policy associated with non-attendance.

She concluded:

The cumulative effect on the framing of public policy associated with non-attendance through the three identified cultures is a powerful legislative and regulatory web which acts as a form of social and educational exclusion for students whose patterns of attendance and behaviour do not meet the current socially constructed norms. For students defined as 'different' (particularly 'culturally different') within such a social construct, the impact can be devastating. The impact, however, is not isolated to the individual. For society, the long-term effect of public policy on non-attendance as a form of social exclusion is potentially far more expensive than provision of resources at school level, either in welfare or detention costs.

4.7

A SOLUTION TO THE PROBLEM?

We asked Jan if she had started out hoping to find a solution. She was adamant that she had not, though it would have been very nice if a solution had emerged. She asked why we were always looking for solutions:

> There will always be truancy. There will always be kids who don't want to go to school and always people who don't want to have some of them in school. There'll never be a solution. Given that we've got all this legislation, we could look at it in a negative sense and say 'We've got this legislation and so we can do this, this and this.' Or we could say 'Well, given we've got this problem, why don't we look at it in a conciliatory way and say "We've got to look at things in a different way, an inclusive way, not a way which excludes a whole type of child that I would call 'different'."'

We asked about the rights of children to education and the fact that no government would be willing to say 'Education's here but you don't need to take it if you don't want to. Suit yourself'. She agreed, and knew that some children who wanted an education needed the protection of the law to get access to it. But she wanted to see how it *could* work so that it was a positive rather than a negative approach:

I knew from my experience in school that it was often a way of getting rid of problems rather than trying to address them. In the end it always came down to priorities and attitude, lack of resources and lack of pedagogical knowledge of how to approach a difficult bunch of students who were different. If there are going to be fundamental changes, they will have to come at grassroots level and that means the teachers will need the resources to be able to implement them.

On the evidence of her findings, Jan saw little evidence of willingness to change resourcing priorities in order to help teachers to cope with difficult and truanting school students, nor to take steps to change preconceived notions about difference, responsibility and social justice. She knew how difficult that would be to achieve. Even so, she considered the difficulties should not be an excuse for inaction. Her experience of interviewing, observing, participating in a whole range of activities had given her clues as to how fundamental changes in attitude might be achieved, in time.

As she saw it, they would involve a move from the punitive culture to the culture of mediation; from the culture of dependence to the culture of natural justice; the culture of difference to the culture of awareness; from 'truancy' to 'non-attendance'. All these interlinked cultures would still lead to legislative and regulatory frameworks, but frameworks of a different kind. They would lead not to the culture of rejection and exclusion but to the culture of inclusion and equity.

Pie in the sky? Jan was confident that it was not. She provided a lengthy list of ways in which a culture of mediation might be achieved over time through increased community cultural awareness. That included items such as the incorporation of the principles of natural justice into school decision-making processes; the rights of individuals and parents involved in suspension and exclusion processes to be made aware of ways of challenging decisions; decreased reliance on the justice system; more effective inter-agency action; decreased dependence on suspension and exclusion as a form of behaviour management; more resources and more flexible notions of 'school'. All that and much more, some of which, as she knew, would be likely to raise hackles and set up resistance. She also knew that she was on dangerous ground by drawing attention to differences. She knew that if all her ideas were introduced in one large batch, in all probability they would be dismissed as impossible to implement or too expensive. Old beliefs would harden and any idea of fundamental change would receive a setback. However, she genuinely believed, and still does, that it should be possible to start from small beginnings – and small beginnings would be better than continuation of the status quo which, on the basis of previous experience, will never work.

 **4.8**

DISCUSSION

It's not easy to carry out an ethnographic study, particularly when the topic deals with sensitive areas, and Jan knew that locating key individuals, obtaining access to materials, institutions and organizations would require careful negotiation and consideration. And it would require time. She did not embark on the topic without extensive consultation, discussion with colleagues, reading about ways other research had been carried out and discussing pitfalls with ethnographers who had successfully completed and reported on their investigations. She was committed to her topic which, as we have said, involved the search for meaning and it seemed to her, and to her advisers, that the ethnographic approach was the best, and probably the only way for the investigation to proceed. So on reflection, was that the best way to explore meaning and belief systems?

The three research questions

You'll recall that she started with three basic questions, which were:

- In what ways has a particular view of truancy produced specific perceptions and responses to youth and compulsory education?

- What cultural factors have influenced popular and academic beliefs about truancy?
- In what ways have these responses influenced the creation and enactment of public policy associated with truancy?

It seems to us that these questions, devised early in the research planning together with the many sub-questions which developed as the research progressed, have held up well. Everything in her thesis was directed towards investigating and answering them. She used them as a framework for the study and kept returning to them to make sure she was still following the same trail. It's easy to wander, to become interested in other topics which are side shoots of the original and to forget what the focus of the study is.

Reflexivity

Over the years, there have been many criticisms of ethnography on the grounds that it lacks reliability, validity and objectivity; that it is not systematic, involves the researcher too closely as an active participant and, some would say, is little more than journalism. No doubt the arguments about what ethnography is or is not and what its strengths and weaknesses are will continue to exercise minds, even among ethnographers themselves. In Brewer's view, the emergence of reflexivity as an issue in ethnographic research goes some way to address some of these issues:

> We are encouraged to be reflexive in our account of the research process, the data collected and the way we write up, because reflexivity shows the partial nature of our representation of reality and the multiplicity of competing versions of reality.
>
> (Brewer 2000: 129)

It's probably impossible for ethnographic researchers to be completely neutral, though as Fetterman (1998: 22) advises, they 'can guard against the more obvious biases by making them explicit'. Jan regarded analytical reflexivity as an essential stage in her research. She felt she had to stand back, to consider her personal impact on the data and to consider the extent to which her value judgements might influence the way she interpreted and wrote about the data. She was so closely involved in and committed to her topic that it would have been difficult, if not impossible, to eliminate elements of bias entirely, but we think she succeeded in most respects and her reflexive approach went a long way to legitimize her findings.

The promise of confidentiality and anonymity

We asked whether she felt confident she had been able to honour that promise and she felt she had done everything in her power to guarantee both. She never divulged what had been said in interviews unless the interviewees gave permission. The four SWOs were interested to know what the others had said, but she never told them. She never divulged information she knew to be confidential but sometimes interviewees played games with her by asking questions in committees about issues they had earlier discussed with her 'in confidence'. They knew she knew their views but were using that particular stratagem to ensure the public airing of their particular concerns. That could have been awkward but there was generally somebody in the committee who responded and so the individuals concerned got their desired airings.

She was particularly careful about ensuring that comments made by some of the truants could never be traced. She used some of their views as examples of opinions of alienated youth but in ways which gave no possible indication of where they came from nor who they were.

She found it disconcerting that some of her interviewees made guesses, not about individuals but about which district she was discussing. When they were fishing for confirmation, they would announce in committees that 'obviously you were talking about district 1 (2, 3 or 4) here', but she never rose to the challenge. Sometimes they were right, though not always, and she decided there was nothing she could have done about the good guessers.

So what did she learn from her research experience?

She described the entire study as a process of learning, discovering, adapting, adjusting boundaries, interpreting and looking for meaning. During that process, she learnt a lot about research, her topic and her own resilience and, although it took a long time, she finally did begin to understand that elusive culture of compulsion.

She recalled the stage when she believed she would never be able to see the full picture. The diagrams helped to clarify her thoughts and in the end it all seemed so obvious. She couldn't imagine why she hadn't seen it before!

She got better at a whole lot of things, including interviewing. As the interviewing went on, she became more focused and able to move from the factual to a level of abstraction. She recalled that she knew from previous experience that she had to be systematic about everything she did and mostly she was, even when she was in a fog. The overload problems rather overwhelmed her at several stages but she still did her utmost to be organized about the way she did things because she knew how terrible it would be if she let things slip.

We asked whether, on reflection, she felt she could have done anything better. In spite of all her efforts to manage the information efficiently, she felt she could have produced a better indexing and cross-referencing system. She didn't feel she would have learnt any more by collecting more data but she thought she might have been able to get more out of the data she had if the system had worked better. Though she was pleased with some chapters, she was confident she could have done better with others. If she had had more time, she thought her writing would have improved, but the problem with research is that there never is enough time.

She is now a full-time university lecturer and roles have been reversed because she has responsibility for supervising research students herself. We asked what advice she would give to any of her student researchers who were hoping to carry out an ethnographic investigation. She had definite views:

I would tell any Masters students that though it's perfectly possible to make use of ethnographic methods and techniques, it would be impossible to achieve the degree of immersion necessary in the time allowed for a Masters degree in order to be able to develop an understanding of how a culture works. Ethnography takes time and you can't hurry understanding.

As far as doctoral students are concerned, I would say 'OK, but only as long as you understand what will be involved, you are sufficiently committed to the topic and already have some experience in qualitative research.' I would discourage them from going out into the field until they'd developed a structure of their own from which to work. I'd ask them to reflect, often and vocally, on what they were doing and why they were doing it that way. I think I was quite successful in focusing on why interviewees were doing things one way rather than another but, looking back, I don't think I was very good about focusing on myself and questioning why *I* did things in a certain way. I'd try to help students to avoid that and to talk about it.

Shortage of time or not, in the end everything worked exceptionally well and Jan produced a thesis which was awarded a university prize 'for outstanding scholarship in postgraduate research'.

FURTHER READING

Ethnography

If any ethnographers happen to read what we have written about ethnography, they will no doubt have several fits about the way we have oversimplified this complex concept. However, here we have been concerned only with those aspects which relate in some way to Jan's thesis. A great deal has been written and anyone considering an ethnographic study will no doubt wish to read widely in order to be informed about all the many and varied interpretations of what ethnography is – and what it is not. You might wish to start with the following:

Brewer, John D. (2000) *Ethnography*. Buckingham: Open University Press.
   Chapters of particular interest include Chapter 1 (What is ethnography?); Chapter 3 (The research process in ethnography) and Chapter 4 (The analysis, interpretation and presentation of ethnographic data). The section on reflexivity (pp. 126–33) is also well worth reading, as is his section on gatekeepers (p. 83). And there's a glossary of terms, which helps.
Denscombe, Martyn (1998) *The Good Research Guide*. Buckingham: Open University Press.
   In Chapter 5, pp. 68–81, Denscombe provides a very readable and understandable account of ethnography which he discusses under the headings of 'Ethnography as a topic and as description'; 'Ethnography and theory'; 'Ethnographers as part of the world they seek to describe'; 'Putting the researcher's "self" into ethnographic research'.

There is a brief but particularly good section on the issue of reflexivity. Chapter 5 also provides guidance on access to fieldwork settings and the advantages and disadvantages of ethnography. A checklist is provided.

Interviews

Bell, Judith (1999) *Doing Your Research Project: A Guide for First-time Researchers in Education and Social Science*, 3rd edn. Buckingham: Open University Press.

Chapter 9, pp. 135–6, 'Planning and conducting interviews', provides guidance on type of interview, bias, recording and verification, time, place and style of the interview. The chapter ends with a checklist and suggestions for further reading.

Cohen, L. and Manion, L. (1994) *Research Methods in Education*, 4th edn. London: Routledge.

Chapter 13, pp. 271–98, 'The interview', provides sound advice about planning, conditions, features of the research interview, procedures – and problems.

Fidler, B. (1992) 'Telephone interviewing' reprinted as Chapter 19 in N. Bennett, R. Glatter and R. Levačić (1994) *Improving Educational Management through Research and Consultancy*. London: Paul Chapman.

May, T. (1993) 'Interviewing: methods and process', Chapter 6 in *Social Research: Issues, Methods and Process*. Buckingham: Open University Press.

The management of information

Baker, Sally (1999), Chapter 5, pp. 64–88, 'Finding and searching information sources, in J. Bell, *Doing Your Research Project: A Guide for First-time Researchers in Education and Social Science* provides useful information and cautionary tales about the misrecording of biographical details.

Brewer, John D. (2000) *Ethnography*. Buckingham: Open University Press., Chapter 4, pp. 108–22, deals with patterns and categories, data management, index coding and classification systems.

Orna, E. with Stevens, G. (1995) *Managing Information for Research*. Buckingham: Open University Press.

This is an invaluable book based on Elizabeth Orna's years of experience of working with students undertaking research in a variety of disciplines. Worth consulting.

Qualitative data analysis

Brewer, John D. (2000) *Ethnography*. Buckingham: Open University Press. Chapter 4, 'The analysis, interpretation and presentation of ethnographic data', pp. 104–26, deals with the various stages in ethnographic data analysis, computer-assisted data analysis and interpretation in a clear way. Very helpful.

Denscombe, M. (1998) *The Good Research Guide for Small-scale Social Research Projects*. Buckingham: Open University Press.

Chapter 11, pp. 207–23, 'Qualitative data', discusses procedures for analysing qualitative data, early coding and categories, identification of themes and relationships and includes information about computer-aided analysis of qualitative data.

Hammersley, M. (1990) *Classroom Ethnography: Empirical and Methodological Essays*. Buckingham: Open University Press.

Chapter 7, 'Measurement in ethnography: the case of Pollard on teaching style', deals with the problem of measurement in ethnographic research. The various ways in which ethnographers offer evidence in support of their claims are discussed – and the problems associated with measurement.

Pages 112–13, 'Selection of indicators', raise the issue of making linkages between concepts and data.

Miles, M.B. and Huberman, A.M. (1994) *Qualitative Data Analysis*, 2nd edn. Thousand Oaks, CA: Sage.

Everything in this excellent book is worth reading, particularly pp. 5–9 of the Introduction and Chapter 4, pp. 50–89, 'Early steps in analysis'.

Writing

Bell, Judith (1999) Chapter 13, 'Writing the report', deals with getting started, structuring the report, the need for revision, plagiarism and evaluating your own research.

May, T. (1993) In pp. 128–9, 'Writing ethnography', May gives eight good suggestions on writing on ethnography most of which, as he says, could apply equally well to other methods.

Miles and Huberman (1994) again. Chapter 12, pp. 298–306, 'Producing reports', is helpful and includes guidance about style, formats and structures. Quite apart from the quality of their own writing and the amount of useful information they provide, we like their sense of humour. The opening sentence of this chapter states that 'qualitative research is not just an exercise for our private enjoyment'. Right. In the end we have to account for ourselves and justify our conclusions.

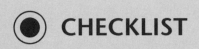

CHECKLIST

1 As always, permission has to be given before you can begin your research.	Make sure you explain exactly what you wish to find out, what access you will need to people and materials and what you propose to do with your findings.
2 Read as much as you can about your topic before you even think about data collecting.	You need to discover all you can about the current state of knowledge in your field. Always be on the lookout for key issues, likely themes and categories.
3 It's not enough in your review of the literature just to list what you have read (the furniture sale catalogue).	You will need to discriminate, to select only what is relevant to your topic, to comment on conflicting views and to summarize.
4 Produce an index system (sometimes known as index coding) which incorporates ways of cross-referencing.	You need to be able to identify quotations, categories and possible themes quickly and easily.
5 You can't select methods of data collection until you're absolutely sure what it is you want to find out.	Sounds obvious but there is always a temptation to 'get on with the research' and to rush into fieldwork before you know where you're going. Keep returning to the purpose of the study. It's easy to wander.

6 Don't launch into fieldwork until you have a possible structure from which to work.	Inevitably there will be changes but collecting data about anything and everything in the hope that something will hit you in the eye is likely to lead you down blind alleys.
7 Devise research questions to guide the progress of the investigation.	Set boundaries. Make sure you will have time to do everything you plan to do – and then allow more, just in case.
8 Don't contemplate an ethnographic study unless you have sufficient time to immerse yourself in the culture of your selected individuals, groups or, as in Jan's case, an entire society.	It's quite possible to use ethnographic techniques and methods in any qualitative study but immersion requires time. Understanding can't be hurried.
9 Define your terms. Truancy may mean different things to different people, as Jan found out.	Imprecision in research is serious.
10 Qualitative analysis may not be an exact science but that's not to say it shouldn't be systematic and rigorous (Brewer 2000: 107).	The quality of the analysis will depend on the structure to which you have worked, the thoroughness of the data collection, the honesty of the data reduction and the accuracy of your reporting.
11 Consider establishing a research contract with your participants, where appropriate.	They are entitled to know what the conditions of your research are. Don't promise more than you can deliver.

12 If you promise anonymity and confidentiality, make sure you define what you mean.	And those promises must always be honoured.
13 Writing starts early in the research.	Transcribe field notes (or at least parts you might possibly wish to use) as soon after the event as possible. Try out your index coding and make sure it works before you go too far. If it doesn't, change the system.
14 Analysis doesn't start once all data are collected.	It's all part of the ongoing process of 'selecting, focusing, simplifying, abstracting and transforming the data that appear in written-up field notes or transcriptions' (Miles and Huberman 1994: 10).
15 Do your best to validate your evidence.	Look for several sources in order to confirm your findings.
16 You can't include all your data in the thesis so you have to select only those parts which are of direct relevance to your topic.	Take care though. Selectivity can distort the evidence if you allow your prejudices to influence what you select and what you reject.
17 Resist the temptation to return to the field unless absolutely necessary.	It can be an excuse to put off the day when you will have to get down to writing.

18 If you've written up as you've gone along, taken care with data reduction, always kept the research questions in mind, triangulated your evidence and have a workable index, writing the final draft of the research should be relatively straightforward.	Put another way, if you haven't, you could be in trouble in sorting out what is important and what isn't from the mountain of paper facing you.
19 If you were thinking of asking, no, we haven't always been able to keep to the rigorous approach we have been suggesting.	But we've learnt that if we are able to keep close to it, it certainly saves a lot of grief.

● Part 5

THE SURVEY

The importance of the topic ● problems of agreed definitions ● looking to the published research ● problems of reliability and validity ● the danger of selectivity and bias ● categorizing findings from the literature ● the research questions ● the content, design and piloting of the staff questionnaire ● the population ● potential biasing factors ● null hypotheses ● Spearman's rho ● chi-square (Pearson's) ● following the analysis trail ● researching at a distance ● discussion of findings.

5.1

BACKGROUND TO
THE STUDY

Introduction

At the time he carried out this doctoral investigation (Chan 2000) Tim was a full-time member of staff at a polytechnic in Singapore. His family and work commitments left him little free time but, like most of the other researchers whose work we have discussed in this book, he decided it was unlikely he ever would have more time. It was to be now or never and so he registered for a part-time PhD at a British university. It took him five hard years of study at a distance and he needed all the determination he could find to keep going at what were sometimes critical professional and family times.

He had for some years been interested in finding ways of identifying and measuring teaching effectiveness and decided to select this topic for his research. His interest in teaching effectiveness stemmed from his exposure to education systems in Western and in Asian settings. He completed his pre-university education in Hong Kong, which is a predominantly Asian society with strong Confucian traditions and where teachers were in general respected by students. To have been evaluated by students would have offended the dignity of many teachers and any negative evaluations could have been interpreted as showing disrespect or causing disgrace to the individuals concerned. So, not unnaturally, student evaluation of teaching (SET) in Hong Kong was, at that time, unheard of.

When he continued his undergraduate and postgraduate studies in Australia and the United Kingdom, he discovered that teachers did not always receive the same respect. In fact, their teaching was increasingly subject to observation, scrutiny and evaluation and their professionalism could be, and frequently was, questioned by others – including students.

Singapore is also an Asian country, but ever-increasing demands for quality and accountability in higher education institutions had escalated to such a degree that in Tim's polytechnic SET had become a requirement, each department being permitted to select a student evaluation instrument suited to departmental use. Singapore's polytechnics are mainly teaching institutions, research taking second place. Competition among institutions is strong because all wish to attract the best students from a small pool of secondary school leavers and therefore proof of the quality and effectiveness of teaching was, and still is, supremely important. However, many of the student evaluation instruments used originated in Western countries. He writes:

The majority of these instruments were adopted with no modifications. Since the concepts and practices of teaching in this [that is, his own] polytechnic may be different from those in overseas universities where the evaluation instruments were first used, I feel that we may be using an inappropriate set of teaching characteristics as measures of teaching effectiveness. In other words, my observations in the West have led me to question the validity of these instruments and their applicability to our own teaching contexts. I query the underlying assumptions of teaching effectiveness as reflected by the design and content of these instruments.

He therefore decided that the main aim of his study should be:

To discover how academic staff in an Asian setting perceive effective teaching and SET and subsequently to compare their views with those of staff in Western countries.

His first task was to look to the available literature on SET in order to discover what research had already been done. As always, this was a sound step to take.

Consulting the literature

His reading was wide-ranging and so comprehensive that there can be few relevant publications worldwide he did not examine. He was determined that all sources of research into SET should be identified and findings analysed. Like other researchers whose work we have considered earlier in this book, he found it difficult to call a halt to his reading. He accumulated vast amounts of information. Fortunately, he was systematic and, at an early stage in his reading, began to classify and prioritize research findings.

We've mentioned this before, but it's so important that now we're about to mention it again, namely that waiting until all reading has been done before beginning a first-thoughts system of categorizing findings is a recipe for disaster. In the checklist to Part 3 of the book we say that 'If ever you say "Right. Nearly finished. I've collected all the data and all I've got to do now is write it up and sort out the references", you're in trouble'. Similarly, if, at the end of your preliminary allocated time for consulting the literature, you are left facing a desk covered by giant heaps of notes which give you no overall picture of the research relating to your topic, *you are in trouble*. If all your notes and your system of classification are in good shape, much of the hard work of writing a review of the literature will be done. If your notes are stored in a computer file, there are ways of highlighting key issues which will help in the analysis of findings but that in no way removes the need to think in terms of an early system of classification. The computer will not do the job for you. You give the orders and then it does as it's told.

Tim amended his priorities many times throughout his reading and finally produced the following framework for analysis:

- Types of SET instruments used in North America and other Western countries.

- The purposes of SET.
- Academic staff perceptions, beliefs and concerns about SET.
- Student concerns about SET.
- The reliability, validity and biasing effects of SET.
- Peer and administrator evaluation.
- Teachers' self-evaluation.
- Assessment of student learning as an indicator of teacher performance.
- Ways in which SET can be used to improve teaching.

All this and much more, but nowhere could he find an agreed definition of 'effective teaching'. Researchers started from different bases. There were many theories and strongly held beliefs but little overall consensus about – well, practically anything, apart from the following consistently reported findings that:

- 'Effective teaching' is a multi-faceted concept and, particularly where SET is to be used for promotion or tenure purposes, multiple methods of data collection are needed.
- Only an appropriate mechanism or instrument which reliably and validly measures the effectiveness of lecturers *against an identified set of criteria* and which will provide feedback to the lecturer will suffice.

These recommendations sound reasonable enough but producing such an appropriate mechanism or instrument proved to be quite a challenge for Tim when he came to develop his own data-collecting instruments.

The review of the literature

It was impossible for him to include everything in the review and so he had to make a decision about what to select and what to reject, as all researchers do. He was aware of the problems of selectivity and the danger of **bias**, was determined that the selection should be fair and should provide a balanced view of the research findings.

It's impossible for us to provide examples of all the research findings reported in the literature. That would have been a book in itself, and so we've selected just one topic, namely staff perceptions, beliefs and concerns about SET. This was an area of particular importance to him because his pre-research discussions with colleagues had indicated that some were unhappy about students being asked to evaluate their teaching – unhappy on principle, because of some previous experience which gave them no confidence in the exercise or because of anxiety about the purpose of the exercise. He looked to the published research to see whether his colleagues' beliefs and perceptions were similar to those of teachers in different parts of the world and in different contexts and cultures. The following are just a few of the perceptions which were identified:

- Students cannot make consistent judgements concerning instructor effectiveness because of their immaturity and lack of experience.
- Only colleagues with excellent publication records and experience are qualified both to teach and to evaluate their peers' instruction.
- Student rating schemes are nothing more than a popularity contest with the warm, friendly, humorous, easy-grading instructor emerging as the winner every time.
- Students are not able to make accurate judgements concerning either instruction or instructor until they have been away from the course, and possibly away from the institution for several years.
- Student rating forms are both unreliable and invalid.
- Many extraneous variables could affect student rating.
- Grades or marks that the students either expect to receive or actually receive are highly related to their ratings of both the course and the instructor.
- Use of student ratings constricts teaching styles and deters academic staff from exploring and using a variety of teaching methods.

Perceptions and beliefs are one thing, but Tim was looking for evidence from the literature to support or to refute them and reliable evidence was hard to come by. One of the problems he faced was that, in order to accept the findings, he had to assume that the feedback forms used in each of the investigations were well designed and so likely to produce reliable data. That made him uneasy because few of the findings gave details of the context in which the exercise was carried out, nor of the ways in which questionnaires were piloted and validated.

He feared that if teaching staff had experience of completing badly designed 'home made' student rating forms which might not have undergone the statistical procedures necessary in order to construct reliable instruments, then possibly the 'data' produced might well have led them to conclude that their beliefs were justified. He was concerned that many of the reported findings which were presented as valid evidence failed to provide the necessary detail as to how *validity* had been achieved. He was frequently in the position of having to query what he regarded as questionable evidence by making such statements as 'this is not supported by the literature', 'research findings suggest that this perception is not valid', 'research findings and discussion on this issue are contradictory' – and so on. In some cases, trying to compare one investigation with another was like trying to compare apples with pears. However, he was able to conclude that, where researchers had specified which measures of teaching effectiveness were selected, the research appeared to be *reliable*. You will recall that 'reliability' is the extent to which a test or procedure produces similar results under similar conditions on different occasions. It was more difficult to come to any conclusions about their *validity*, which is an altogether more complex concept. It tells us whether an item measures or describes what it is supposed to measure or describe (though also see Denscombe 1998: 213–14; Sapsford and Jupp 1996: 1–23; and Bell 1999: 103–5). He found similar difficulty over the lack of an agreed definition of *bias*. Though many research reports claimed that steps had been taken to eliminate it, there appeared to be no agreement about what it actually was. One definition was that 'it is a circumstance that unduly influences teachers' ratings', but that proved to be difficult to test. Another was that 'student ratings are biased to the extent that they are influenced by variables that are unrelated to teaching effectiveness', but that definition also seemed to be inadequate. It was difficult for Timothy to obtain what he regarded as firm evidence of many of the issues because of the size, complexity and conflicting results of the many investigations into SET. Even so, after filtering the very large number of items relating to staff perceptions of SET, he felt sufficiently confident to state that

> In general, stated reasons for academic staff opposing SET are related to issues such as their attitude towards academic freedom, their perceptions of the representativeness and accuracy of what is evaluated, their conception of the immaturity of students, their sensitivity to student feedback and their values with respect to the institution's system of rewards and incentives. The research literature points out that many of these commonly held negative perceptions and beliefs concerning student ratings are, on the whole, myths or misconceptions. On the contrary, considerable evidence supporting the credibility of students as evaluators of instruction in higher education has emerged from past research.

We have not included his references to the sources on which he drew, though there were many, but he made no claims which were not supported by what he regarded as reliable research findings, even though he felt obliged to use terminology such as 'in general' and 'on the whole'.

What did he learn from his study of the literature?

In spite of the difficulties he encountered throughout his analysis of the literature, he learnt a great deal about the processes involved in focusing and classifying the research findings. The experience was useful because it gave him ideas about and practice in the management of large amounts of information and alerted him to likely pitfalls and possible ways of structuring his own research. It taught him to be careful about accepting research findings at face value when inadequate information had been provided about methods of data collection and analysis. His study of the literature enabled him to understand the complexity of

SET research, the importance of designing, piloting and testing instruments and identifying which approaches were likely to lead to reliable and valid conclusions – and in his view, that made the whole exercise worthwhile. However, several major concerns remained, the first of which was that the investigations into SET which he had examined were based on educational settings in the USA, the UK and Australia. He found no research which considered the suitability of those Western SET instruments to educational institutions in Asian settings. If that were not known, he felt strongly that his polytechnic might continue to carry out student evaluations 'blindly' and then use the results for decision making.

He remained anxious to discover whether students felt as uneasy about making critical comments on staff teaching as he had been when he was a pre-university student in Hong Kong. The accessibility of television, films and the Internet had to a large extent opened up the world and the ways of the world. Attitudes might have changed, but what if they had not? What if respect for teachers still made students unwilling to make any comments which might be considered disrespectful? If so, that could invalidate the entire process. There was so much to find out and to test.

He needed to discover how academic staff in Singapore perceived SET in order to be able to compare their perceptions with those of staff in Western countries. That required him to develop a feedback instrument which would

- determine the desirable teaching characteristics of polytechnic lecturers in an institution which emphasized the quality of teaching as a core value;
- identify staff and students' perceptions of the appropriateness of SET in the context of a tertiary educational institution in Singapore;
- determine the reliability and validity of the feedback instrument.

This was a start but each item had to be further broken down into many subdivisions in order to investigate this complex topic, as you will see when we consider the questionnaires later on.

5.2

THE PREPARATION AND
PLANNING

We always have to remember that it is the purpose of the study which determines the methods to be used, not the other way round, and so in this chapter we shall consider some of the steps Tim took in preparing and planning his research programme. He had obtained permission to carry out the research long before he began to make any firm plans. Once the permission was given, he was able to consider the various ways in which his topic might be developed. His first step was to construct six research questions which he preferred to word in the form of statements, in order to provide a structure for the investigation, which were:

The research questions

R1 To identify the most important characteristics of effective teaching as perceived by academic staff of three departments.

R2 To discover if staff of the three departments (named A, B and C) differ in their perceptions of the most important characteristics of effective lecturers.

R3 To investigate the influence of academic staff background variables on their perceptions of the characteristics of effective lecturers. The background variables include gender, age, rank, years of teaching experience, academic qualifications, formal training in pedagogy and involvement in research and development work.

R4 To investigate whether staff of the three departments consider that students can make meaningful judgements of lecturers when students use the characteristics of effective teaching as a basis for judgement.

R5 To determine if staff from the three departments differ in their perceptions of the appropriateness for students to evaluate lecturers on the perceived five most important characteristics.

R6 To identify the most and least important characteristics of effective lecturers as perceived by staff of the three academic departments.

Punch reminds us that research questions do five main things:

- They organize the project and give it direction and coherence.
- They delimit the project, showing its boundaries.
- They keep the researcher focused during the project.
- They provide a framework for writing up the project.
- They point to the data that will be needed.

(Punch 1998: 38)

We shall be referring to these research questions throughout our discussion of his investigation. His next step was to find his participants.

The population

Two populations were targeted, the first being the full-time academic staff of three polytechnic departments which we have named A, B and C. These departments were chosen because they existed in all four polytechnics in Singapore, because they recruited the highest proportion of academic staff in the polytechnic education sector in Singapore, and because staff of these departments had long experience of using student evaluation as part of their course monitoring exercises. Only full-time academic staff were invited to participate.

The second population was the full-time students of Department B. It should perhaps be mentioned here that anonymity and confidentiality were promised to all participants. They were not asked to give their names, so neither he nor anyone else would have been able to tell who completed which questionnaire.

The questionnaires

During the course of his preparation, he interviewed and talked to many colleagues and had originally hoped to include not only questionnaires, but also staff and student interviews in his research plan. However, he came to the conclusion that it would have been impossible to find the resources to interview large numbers of his participants. He was right. He was an individual researcher and though he had good support from his polytechnic, that did not include financial support or time allowance. His sample was very large, his plans were ambitious and so, with his supervisor's agreement, he decided that questionnaires were the only feasible way of collecting the necessary data.

His first step was to develop two draft questionnaires, one for students and one for full-time members of academic staff, each of which was divided into four parts. *We only have the space to consider the staff questionnaire* but the student questionnaire included many of the same items and was similarly detailed.

Earlier in the book, we considered only a selection of the data-collecting methods and instruments used by Helen, Gilbert, Cher Ping and Jan. However, we have decided to include all four parts of Tim's staff questionnaire here because each one raises interesting issues relating to design, development and analysis.

Each went through many drafts before he was satisfied that all comments, observations and suggestions for improvement had been noted and amendments made but a final pilot study was also needed in order to 'assess the adequacy of the research design and of the instruments to be used for data collection' (Wilson 1996: 103).

The pilot study

As we have said many times in this book and make no apology for doing so again, pilot studies are not optional: they are essential. Although they are necessarily small, they should as far as possible involve respondents who are different from, though as close as possible to, those who are to be asked to complete the final versions of the questionnaires. Five staff 'volunteers' were recruited, one of whom had been teaching in the polytechnic for more than ten years, two for between five and ten years and two fewer than five years. Two were female and three male and they came from different departments. They were asked to complete all four parts of the staff and student questionnaires, to comment on and suggest any necessary modifications. They were particularly asked to comment on the *content validity* of the questions in order to be sure they adequately covered the content or area of concern being considered. In other words, had he omitted any essential aspects which related to the topic on the questionnaires? Finally, a round table discussion was held in order to obtain feedback and suggestions for modifications were incorporated into the design of the questionnaire.

Distribution and return of the questionnaire

The questionnaire was distributed personally to the academic staff of two of the three departments and by the head of department of the third department. Completed questionnaires were either returned personally by the participants (hand delivered to Tim) or returned through internal mail.

Staff response rate

166 questionnaires were distributed to full-time staff of the three departments and 108 (60.84 per cent) were returned. Seven of the 108 were incomplete and were set aside as unusable. The remaining 101 questionnaires were analysed for the study. As we

have said, we are only considering the staff questionnaire, but to give you an idea of the overall size of the investigation, 697 questionnaires were distributed to the students, 565 of which were returned. 14 were incomplete and were unusable and so the analysis was based on the 551 (79.05 per cent) usable returns. This was quite an undertaking.

5.3

THE STAFF QUESTIONNAIRE

Tim knew precisely what information he needed in order to address his six research questions. Not everyone can claim to be so clear-headed but you have to remember that he had spent a great deal of necessary time on preliminary studies, refining his topic and eliminating irrelevancies – and that investment of time paid dividends. We have spoken of 'the staff questionnaire' but in fact it has four main parts and three more subsections. They cover:

1 Staff background.
2 Characteristics of effective teaching:
   • Characteristics of effective teaching considered appropriate for students to evaluate.
   • Characteristics of effective teaching and their associated dimensions of teaching.
   • Staff perceptions of the five most and least important characteristics of effective teaching.
3 Staff confidence in the means of evaluation likely to be effective in improving teaching.
4 Potential biasing factors which may affect the reliability of student evaluation of teaching.

This is a very long questionnaire and Tim knew that his respondents were doing him a favour in agreeing to participate. He also knew they would become impatient if the items were too complex and the questionnaire badly designed. So look critically at each of the four parts as if you were one of the respondents. Keep the research questions in mind and ask yourself which parts relate to which research questions. If you have had experience of designing questionnaires, you will know how taxing it is to get everything exactly right, so could you have done it better? If so, how?

Staff background

Table 10   Staff background (Please circle your answer)

1	Department	1	A
		2	B
		3	C
2	Gender	1	Male
		2	Female
3	Age	1	Below 30 years
		2	30–40 years
		3	Above 40 years
4	Academic rank	1	Principal lecturer
		2	Senior lecturer
		3	Lecturer
5	Teaching experience in the polytechnic	1	< 5 years
		2	5–10 years
		3	> 10 years
6	Highest qualification	1	PhD
		2	Masters
		3	Bachelor
7	Have you completed any courses in teaching and learning (e.g. MEd, BEd, DipEd, Cert Ed, TMC, CT, ACT etc.)?	1	Yes
		2	No
8	Are you currently involved in research and development work (e.g. academic research, industrial project development, etc.)?	1	Yes
		2	No

Any views about this questionnaire?
As far as you can judge, are all the items really necessary, or do

some of them just clutter up the questionnaire? Tim decided he needed them all because he had to discover whether staff background in any way influenced their view of SET.

How long do you think it would have taken respondents to complete? Two minutes? Less? More?

Questionnaires have to be quick and easy to complete or respondents will lose patience and throw them into the bin. If you want readily available factual information, it's wise to keep questions and methods of responding as simple as possible and that is what Timothy did. If there are any items which respondents may not remember without checking records, the odds are that the questionnaire will be put to one side until they have a minute to spare. They are likely to be busy people and there never are minutes to spare in a packed working day. It will get further and further under the pile of essential things to be done yesterday until eventually it becomes another candidate for the bin.

Will everybody have understood what is needed?

Will they all know how to respond? Tim's early and ongoing discussions, consultations, trials with colleagues and his final pilot study produced no problems, but what do you think?

Does he take account of how the data will be recorded and analysed?

Respondents were asked to circle a number (a code) which seems simple enough and required no particular thought or checking of records – unless they happened to have forgotten how old they were or whether they were male or female. Because responses could only be one of two or three, it was perfectly safe to code beforehand (see pp. 22–5).

Is there likely to be any item which respondents might consider to be too personal, sensitive and/or offensive?

Some people feel rather delicate about being asked to say how old they are, but the age range (below 30 years, 30–40 years and above 40 years) is surely broad enough to avoid any offence, isn't it?

What about appearance?

Does it look like a professionally prepared questionnaire or something unchecked and thrown together in five minutes? Looks good to us, but what do you think?

* * *

Appearance is important but prettiness is not enough. It has to be useful and fit for Tim's purpose so did the questionnaire produce any useful or interesting information?

Table 11   Summary of staff background data

Staff background		Frequency	Percentage
Department	A	36	35.6
	B	34	33.7
	C	31	30.7
Gender	Male	55	54.5
	Female	46	45.5
Age	Below 30 years	9	8.9
	30–40 years	70	69.3
	Above 40 years	22	21.8
Rank	Principal lecturer	2	2.0
	Senior lecturer	10	9.9
	Lecturer	89	88.1
Teaching experience	< 5 years	36	35.6
	5–10 years	38	37.6
	> 10 years	27	26.7
Higher qualification	Doctorate	60	0.0
	Master	0	59.4
	Bachelor	41	40.6
Completed teaching	Yes	68	67.3
and learning course	No	33	32.7
Involved in R	Yes	26	25.7
and D work	No	75	74.3

This table provides a picture of staff demography and sets the scene. There's not much more to say about these descriptive statistics at this stage, apart from the fact that the majority of staff are relatively young, are well qualified (almost 60 per cent having Masters degrees) and 67.3 per cent have completed teaching and learning courses. As we have said, Singapore polytechnics are mainly teaching institutions, research taking second place, but even so 67.3 per cent is a commendable proportion compared with many other institutions of higher education in the world. So, these data are moderately interesting but, if you refer back to the research questions, you will see that they are a necessary and integral part of each one and are needed for most of the statistical tests which we consider in Chapter 4.

On to the second part of the questionnaire.

Characteristics of effective teaching

Originally, Tim had identified 45 characteristics of effective teaching, selected from those most commonly reported in the literature, from samples taken from feedback instruments provided by several overseas technological universities and from a selection of student evaluation forms used in various departments in the polytechnic.

Members of the final pilot study group were asked to select which of the proposed 45 characteristics listed in the questionnaire they considered to be relevant *in the polytechnic context* and this they did, but all five said they suffered from various degrees of questionnaire fatigue as they worked their way through the list. In their view 45 characteristics were too many. Based on their feedback, the draft was modified and the characteristics were reduced to 21.

Staff respondents were first asked to indicate which of the 21 they considered to be most important characteristics of effective teaching and then to specify which they considered might be appropriate for students to evaluate. Items were listed in random order. (See Table 12.)

Characteristics of effective teaching and their associated dimensions of teaching

Before we move on to the next stage of the 'characteristics' questionnaire, a quick reminder, as always, about the need to consider what will be done with these individual items before there is any question of distribution. Tim claimed to be a 'rookie' educational researcher but he had a Masters degree in auditing

Table 12 Characteristics of effective teaching considered appropriate for students to evaluate
(Please tick 'Yes' if you agree with the statement in the opposite column, put a cross under 'No' if you disagree and a question mark if you don't know or aren't sure).

Item number	Characteristics	Appropriateness		
		Yes	No	Don't know
1	Provides constructive feedback to students.			
2	Is clear and comprehensible in lectures.			
3	Is able to relate theory to practice.			
4	Is well-groomed and appropriately attired.			
5	Provides useful handouts of notes.			
6	Makes students feel welcome in seeking help/advice.			
7	Is friendly and approachable to students.			
8	Shows effort in improving quality of teaching.			
9	Sets appropriate course objectives.			
10	Encourages self-learning.			
11	Is fair in grading.			
12	Assigns homework/readings that contribute to subject understanding.			
13	Is sensitive to the feelings/problems of students.			
14	Publishes articles and presents seminar papers.			
15	Gives structured and organized lectures.			
16	Has a good sense of humour.			
17	Is enthusiastic about the subject.			
18	Is firm on class discipline and management.			
19	Has a strong sense of responsibility.			
20	Ensures subject content is up to date.			
21	Shows a thorough knowledge of the subject.			

when he began his doctoral survey and that must have helped. He was not going to be in the position of scratching his head once all the data had been collected and saying 'What on earth I am going to do with this lot?' He was ready and knew what to do.

Do you recall the way Gilbert identified groupings before he distributed questionnaires to his nursing students (pp. 56–7)? He had 76 items, placed them in random order on the questionnaire but, based on his knowledge of the literature and his own experience, decided he should be able to group findings under the four categories of 'Admission criteria'; 'Curriculum'; 'Industry relevance' and 'Quality of teaching and clinical supervision'. Tim adopted the same approach. He also listed the characteristics in random order, but had previously decided that responses could be categorized under the seven headings of 'Subject mastery'; 'Course design'; 'Delivery of teaching'; 'Assessment and assignment'; 'Rapport'; 'Attitude'; and 'Personality'. He was able to make these decisions about the dimensions of teaching from his own experience, from his reading of the Western research literature, because he had consulted colleagues and because each part of his questionnaire had previously been piloted in eight polytechnic departments and by the final pilot study group. Early identification of likely key topics and categories meant that he had the start of a framework for analysis. He knew which items would fit into which dimensions of teaching.

This categorization of findings is the same process as was followed by all the researchers in this book. As we keep saying, a thousand individual items may be very interesting, individually, but if there is no pattern in sight, what can be done with a disorganized heap of notes and computer printouts of anything and everything? Well, not a lot really.

You might have grouped responses differently. There are always different views about which items fit into which category. For example, is 'Is friendly and approachable' best under 'Rapport' or 'Personality'? Tim had to decide and in his view 'Rapport' was the right place. All researchers have decisions to make and as long as they can be justified, their decision is likely to be good enough. (See Table 13.)

On to the third part of the 'characteristics' questionnaire.

Table 13 Characteristics of effective teaching and their associated dimensions of teaching

Teaching dimension	Item no.	Characteristics of effective Teaching
Subject mastery	3	Is able to relate theory to practice.
	14	Publishes articles and presents seminar papers.
	21	Shows a thorough knowledge of the subject.
Course design	9	Sets appropriate course objectives.
	20	Ensures subject content is up to date.
Delivery of teaching	2	Is clear and comprehensible in lectures.
	5	Provides useful handouts of notes.
	10	Encourages self-learning.
	15	Gives structured and organized lectures.
	18	Is firm on class discipline/management.
Assessment and assignment	1	Provides constructive feedback to students.
	11	Is fair in grading.
	12	Assigns homework that contributes to subject understanding.
Rapport	6	Makes students feel welcome in seeking help/advice.
	7	Is friendly and approachable.
	13	Is sensitive to the feelings/problems of students.
Attitude	8	Shows effort in improving teaching quality.
	17	Is enthusiastic about the subject.
Personality	4	Is well-groomed and appropriately attired.
	16	Has a good sense of humour.
	19	Has a strong sense of responsibility.

Staff perceptions of the five most important and the five least important characteristics of teaching

We shall have more to say about this third part of the 'characteristics' questionnaire in the next chapter but, for now, it's enough just to say that respondents were asked to list the five most and least important characteristics in rank order, which appeared to give them no difficulty. On to the third part of the questionnaire.

Staff confidence in means of evaluation

Tim was interested to know about staff confidence in the effectiveness of certain items as means of improving teaching. He produced a six-point *Likert scale* which asked respondents to indicate which of eight means of evaluation they considered to be the most and the least effective in improving teaching. You will recall Gilbert also used a six-point scale which eliminates the 'don't know', 'no opinions' central point (see pp. 53–4). He periodically reversed the rating scale from item 1 (very strongly agree) to item 6 (very strongly disagree) – just to check his respondents were still awake. Here, Tim has also eliminated the central point and item 1 is now 'least confident' and item 6 'most confident'. It's not a bad idea to change the format from time to time. Remember that all that can be said about this Likert scale is that responses coded as 5 would indicate less confidence than those coded as 6 but more than those coded as 4. Rank order is all that can be inferred, not degree of difference between the various categories.

Table 14 illustrates the design of this part of the questionnaire.

Table 15 summarizes the rank order, mean and standard deviation of responses.

A quick reminder about the *standard deviation* (SD) which is used to summarize dispersion. That is to say it reflects the spread and the degree to which the values differ from the arithmetic mean. The greater the dispersion, the larger the standard deviation as a measure of deviation (see Rose and Sullivan 1996: 96–100;

Table 14 Staff confidence in means of evaluation

Item No.	Means of evaluation	Least confident				Most confident	
1	Review of teaching materials by department/section head	1	2	3	4	5	6
2	Review of teaching materials by peers	1	2	3	4	5	6
3	Class observations by department/section head	1	2	3	4	5	6
4	Class observations by peers	1	2	3	4	5	6
5	Student evaluation	1	2	3	4	5	6
6	Evaluation by graduates/alumni	1	2	3	4	5	6
7	Self-evaluation	1	2	3	4	5	6
8	Student passing/success rate	1	2	3	4	5	6

Table 15 Staff confidence in sources of teaching evaluation

Source of evaluation	Rank	Mean	SD*
Review of teaching materials by peers	1	3.91	1.00
Self-evaluation	2	3.90	1.07
Student evaluation	3	3.66	1.36
Class observation by peers	4	3.52	1.15
Review of teaching materials by department/section head	5	3.21	1.25
Class observations by department/section head	6	3.06	1.26
Student passing/success rate	7	2.83	1.36
Evaluations by graduates/alumni	8	2.82	1.30

Note: * SD = standard deviation

Schofield 1996: 41; Denscombe 1998: 196–7; Bell 1999: 178). These days, even very cheap calculators will carry out the calculation for you, so it's no longer really necessary to work out the SD manually – at least, not if you don't want to. However, as

Table 16 Potential biasing factors
(Please circle the number of the appropriate statement)

1 *Lecturer's age*
   1 Older lecturer gets higher ratings and younger lecturer gets lower ratings.
   2 Older lecturer gets lower ratings and younger lecturer gets higher ratings.
   3 Effect on ratings is minimal.
   4 Not sure.

2 *Lecturer's rank*
   1 Lecturer with a higher rank gets higher ratings and lecturer with a lower rank gets lower ratings.
   2 Lecturer with a higher rank gets lower ratings and lecturer with a lower rank gets higher ratings.
   3 Effect on ratings is minimal.
   4 Not sure.

3 *Lecturer's gender*
   1 Female lecturer receives lower ratings than male lecturers.
   2 Female lecturer receives higher ratings than male lecturers.
   3 Effect on ratings is minimal.
   4 Not sure.

4 *Lecturer's academic qualifications*
   1 Lecturer with a higher degree (doctorate/master) receives lower ratings.
   2 Lecturer with a higher degree (doctorate/masters) receives higher ratings.
   3 Effect on ratings is minimal.
   4 Not sure.

5 *Lecturer's grading policy*
   1 Lecturer who is strict in grading gets higher ratings than one who is lenient in grading.
   2 Lecturer who is strict in grading gets lower ratings than one who is lenient in grading.
   3 Effect on ratings is minimal.
   4 Not sure.

always, it *is* necessary to know what the SD means and when to use it.

Don't give up. Only one more part of the questionnaire to go.

Potential biasing factors which may affect the reliability of SET

In this final part of the questionnaire, respondents were asked for their perceptions of 11 potential biasing factors of SET which had been reported as being significant in some of the research conducted in Western academic settings, namely: lecturers' characteristics, course variables and subject characteristics.

Items 6–11 follow the same format for workload, lecture schedule, class size, level of course, subject and subject difficulty. (See Table 16.)

* * *

In Chapter 4, we shall see how Tim analysed a small part of the questionnaire data. In a Masters dissertation and in appropriate contexts, descriptions might well be sufficient, as they were in Helen's descriptive study of the relationship between occupational students' entry qualifications to their final degree awards (see pp. 13–36), but this was a doctoral thesis and 'finding the reasons for things, events and situations, showing why and how they have come to be what they are' (Punch 1998: 15) was what was needed.

So how did he do it?

5.4

DISCUSSION OF THE FINDINGS

At frequent points in any investigation, it's advisable to return to the research questions and the purpose of the study to make sure you are not straying from the original plan. Tim's question-naire was designed in ways which he hoped would allow him to discover staff respondents' views about effective teaching and SET. His intention then was to compare the outcomes of his own research with the published research on SET which he examined as part of his literature search, to see whether there were any apparent differences between the Western and Asian approaches. In the following sections, we consider just a few of the methods he employed in analysing the data from three main areas, together with some of the more general conclusions.

Following the analysis trail: staff background variables and the five most and least important characteristics of effective teaching

He wished to know whether staff background variables (gender, age, rank etc.) had any influence on staff perceptions of the five most and least important characteristics. Respondents were asked to place the five characteristics in rank order with the following results.

Table 17 Staff perceptions of the five most and least important characteristics

5 most important characteristics	Rank	5 least important characteristics
Is clear and comprehensible in lectures.	1	Publishes articles and presents seminar papers.
Gives structured and organized lectures.	2	Is well-groomed and appropriately attired.
Shows thorough subject knowledge.	3	Has a good sense of humour.
Is enthusiastic about the subject.	4	Is sensitive to the feelings of students.
Has strong sense of responsibility.	5	Gives useful handouts of notes.

In order to test the effect of background variables, he first needed to create eight *null hypotheses* which stated that

There is no significant difference at the 0.05 level among the perceptions of the respondents with reference to the top five perceived most important characteristics of effective teaching based on their:

Department **(H1)**, Gender **(H2)**, Age **(H3)**, Academic rank **(H4)**, Teaching experience **(H5)**, Academic qualification **(H6)**, Possession of pedagogy knowledge **(H7)** and Involvement with R and D work **(H8)**.

These null hypotheses addressed three of the research questions. For example:

H1 related to R2 (which was 'to identify if staff from the three departments differ in their perceptions of the most important characteristics of effective learners'). **H2 to H8** related to R3 ('to investigate the influence of academic staff background variables on their perceptions of the characteristics of effective learners').

We have briefly discussed the purpose of the *null hypothesis* and **significance levels** (*probability*) earlier in the book (pp. 97–8) and in the glossary but that was some time ago so it might be as well to remind ourselves that

> The reason why we have to state our hypothesis in the null form is to allow us to estimate how far above or below zero a difference or relationship can be expected to lie due to random sampling error. The further a difference or relationship is above or below zero, the less chance it has of occurring as a result of random sampling error and the greater chance it has of being statistically significant.
>
> (Cohen and Holliday 1982: 122)

In order to test the relationship between staff background and the ranked characteristics, Tim had to look for an appropriate statistical test. He selected the *Spearman's rank order coefficient* (Spearman's rho, expressed by the Greek letter ρ) which is a test where data are measured on an ordinal scale (that is where ranked scores are involved) and which identifies the amount and significance of a *correlation* between *two* variables.

A Spearman's rho of +1 would indicate perfect agreement between the two sets of ranks (and that would be extremely rare) and the rho of –1 would indicate perfect disagreement (equally rare). More information about Spearman's rho is given in the 'Further reading' section at the end of this Part and in the glossary, if you wish to know more.

See what you think about the findings, which he illustrates in Table 18. At first sight, it looks complicated but don't give up. It provides quite interesting information.

In case the table is not absolutely clear, look again and you will see that Department A correlated with Department B gives a rho of 0.843 and Department A correlated with C gave a rho of 0.829. As a rho of +1 would indicate perfect agreement between two ranks, it might be concluded that 0.843 and 0.829 are sufficiently close to +1 to indicate high correlation between Departments A and B and A and C (the + sign is not usually included in positive correlations). The female/male rho of 0.919 indicates that there was even less difference in the rankings of the five

Table 18 Spearman's rank correlation coefficients
(Spearman's rho)

Data sets	Variables	Rho
Department	A/B	0.843
	A/C	0.829
	B/C	0.810
Gender	Female/Male	0.919
Age	Below 30 years/30–40 years	0.756
	Below 30 years/above 40 years	0.661
	30–40 years/above 40 years	0.871
Teaching experience	Less than 5 years/5–10 years	0.887
	Less than 5 years/more than 10 years	0.829
	5–10 years/more than 10 years	0.936
Staff rank	Senior/Junior	0.939
Academic qualification	Masters/Bachelors	0.887
Training in teaching and learning (T and L)	With/without training in T and L	0.806
R and D involvement	With/without R and D involvement	0.800

most important characteristics of effective teaching between male
and female respondents.

These overall high positive values of Spearman's rho enabled
Tim to be confident that there was no significant difference at
the 0.05 level among the perceptions of the respondents with
reference to the top five perceived most important characteristics of effective teaching based on the eight staff background
variables – and so the null hypotheses were accepted. He was
then able to summarize by saying that

> The data suggest that this strong agreement is maintained
> (that is staff agreement on the rank order of the five most
> important characteristics) even when different variables, such
> as departments, gender, age groups, teaching experience, staff
> ranks, academic qualifications, possession of pedagogical
> knowledge and involvement in research and development
> work are studied.

Note the use of 'suggest'. Correlation coefficients are about probability, not about proof, as Gilbert made clear in the discussion of students' perceptions of their diploma course which we discussed in Part 2 of the book.

* * *

Continuing the analysis trail: staff perceptions of students' appropriateness for evaluating teaching effectiveness

In Chapter 1, we listed some concerns about SET which Tim had identified in the published research carried out in Western countries and he was anxious to discover the extent to which those perceptions were common among his own research participants. He decided the findings would be more reliable if he had more than the five characteristics with which to work. Remember that ease of response to the questionnaire items was of great importance. Staff were willing to rank the five most and least important characteristics, but to have been asked to list the top and bottom ten might have been quite another matter. That would have required thought, would have taken time and might well have been put into the 'Too hard' file or more likely into the ever-present bin. Timothy knew that and so devised a relatively simple way of calculating the weighted average score of each most important and least important ranked characteristics which allowed him to produce ranks for all 21 of the characteristics of effective teaching. The purpose of the weighted average was to enable him to rank the characteristics in the order of importance, as rated by respondents (see weighted averages in the 'Further reading' section). The higher the weighted average score of a characteristic, the higher the ranking. Table 19 illustrates the rankings, with 1 being the highest.

Once the calculations were made, Tim was able to produce his list of ten most important characteristics as ranked by staff respondents, but there was one further step in this stage of his analysis. He wanted to know the extent to which those ranked scores were reflected in respondents' views of which characteristics

Table 19 Weighted average of the most important characteristics of effective teaching

Characteristics	Rank	WA score
Is clear and comprehensible in lectures.	1	3.49
Gives structured and organized lectures.	2	2.43
Shows a thorough knowledge of the subject.	3	1.91
Is enthusiastic about the subject.	4	1.22
Has a strong sense of responsibility.	5	0.85

Table 20 Staff perceptions of the appropriateness of students to evaluate lecturers on the ten most important characteristics of effective teaching

Teaching dimension	Characteristics	Rank *	Appro %**
Delivery	Is clear and comprehensible in lectures	1	100
Delivery	Gives structured and organized lectures	2	91
Subject mastery	Shows thorough subject knowledge	3	81
Attitude	Is enthusiastic about the subject	4	91
Personality	Has strong sense of responsibility	5	80
Course design	Ensures subject content is current	6	59
Rapport	Welcomes students who seek help	7	90
Course design	Sets appropriate course objectives	8	70
Delivery	Gives useful handouts of notes	9	78
Delivery	Firm on class discipline	10	95

Notes: * = the rank given by staff to their view of the most important characteristics of effective teaching.
Appro %** = the percentage of staff who considered students to be appropriate in rating lecturers on the corresponding characteristics.

of lecturers were appropriate for students to evaluate: Table 20 presents the picture.

It was no doubt pleasing to Tim to see that the majority of respondents considered students were able to judge a lecturer's teaching effectiveness on the ten most important characteristics, but what he did not know from these results was whether there were any significant distinctions between different departments.

Departmental differences

Once again, he had to find a statistical test which would allow him to ascertain whether there was a relationship between the variables or whether the relationship could reasonably have arisen by chance. He decided to calculate the *chi-square* at the 0.05 level of probability, the starting point for which was again a null hypothesis which related to R5 ('to determine if staff from the three departments differ in their perceptions of the appropriateness for students to evaluate lecturers on the perceived five most important characteristics'). This null hypothesis stated that

> there was no significant difference at the 0.05 level between departments as to staff perceptions of the appropriateness for students to evaluate lecturers on the ten most important characteristics.

Calculating chi-square (X^2) manually would have been tiresome but was quick and easy by computer. The results showed that the chi-square of nine of the ten characteristics (those ranked 1, 2, 3, 4, 5, 7, 8, 9 and 10) indicated that there was no significant difference among academic staff of the three departments (A, B and C) who participated in the research and so the null hypothesis was accepted. Only one characteristic had chi-square values significant at the 0.05 level, namely 'ensures subject content is up to date' (ranked 6) which did show significant differences between departments as to students' ability to make judgements about whether lecturers were up to date. So, the null hypothesis was rejected in this case.

If you look back at Table 20, you will see that item 6 was given the lowest percentage (59 per cent) by respondents but Tim discovered that this percentage hid the wide departmental differences for this particular characteristic. Department A showed the highest percentage (82 per cent) but Departments B and C had percentages of 58 per cent and 35 per cent respectively.

These results clearly demonstrate that accepting descriptive data analysis can in some cases be misleading. It would have been easy for Tim to settle for producing a table which provided a list or groups of responses to the '21 characteristics' items, but he needed to go further and then further still. Each step he took provided greater insight into the variation of view about which characteristics were appropriate for students to evaluate effective teaching. And he was able to move from the descriptive to the inferential level because he was clear about the purpose of this study and his questionnaires were sufficiently well planned, worded and structured in order to produce data in the form which was capable of more complex analysis. It would have been of little consequence that he was statistically competent and knew which applications would be appropriate if his questionnaires had been slapdash and inadequately piloted and if little thought had been given to how the data might be analysed.

The way to get more out of data will always be to make sure the planning and the data collecting instruments are up to the job.

What else did he do?

Well, a great deal. We have not even mentioned the student questionnaire which was distributed to the 697 students and produced a remarkable return of 79.05 per cent of usable returns. We didn't have the space, though we do draw on some of the students' results when we discuss the comparison between staff and student perceptions of the five most and least important characteristics of effective teaching.

Tim used many more statistical tests than we have mentioned to identify differences between two or more variables, all of which involved more and more detail. Whether there was too much detail depended on his and his supervisor's point of view and, of even greater importance, the views of his examiners. The fact that his thesis was accepted without requirements for changes or even for correction of typographical or other errors says much for its quality.

If we had tried to include all his tests, we should need another two or three books to accommodate them. Some of the findings were inconclusive, which was probably inevitable, but we did feel we should very briefly summarize the findings of two main issues which he had identified as being of particular importance, namely:

• the consistency and stability of SET results and the appropriateness of students to evaluate teaching; and
• differences and similarities between the Western and Asian approach to SET.

The consistency and stability of the polytechnic SET results and the appropriateness of students to evaluate teaching

Establishing the consistency and stability of SET was important to him. If lecturers had a certain overall rating in one semester, were they likely to get the same rating in the next semesters? He knew that if he could demonstrate that the results were stable, that would provide support for his claims about the *reliability* of student evaluations.

He compared the overall ratings of 36 lecturers who were evaluated in three successive semesters by different students and discovered that students consistently rated the same lecturer in the same way on different occasions. That is, they were reliable, but they did not demonstrate that the student evaluations were valid.

He carried out further analyses by asking for volunteers to test the correlation between student and peer evaluations which demonstrated that those lecturers who received high student ratings also received high scores when they were evaluated by their peers. In other words, the strong positive correlation between student and peer evaluations supported the *validity* of the *questionnaire-based student evaluation*.

This is important because it enabled Timothy to have confidence in saying that 'the students in the study demonstrated that they were competent to rate their lecturers' – and that one statement allowed him to challenge many of the reasons for staff resistance to SET.

Differences between Western and Asian approaches to SET

Some useful discoveries were made, one of which related to the third part of the questionnaire which asked respondents to rank their degree of confidence in the teaching improvement potential of eight sources of evaluation. Respondents' data were compared with those of research conducted in Western countries. You will recall that one of his key issues was the importance of discovering whether there were differences between the Western and Asian approach to SET and, throughout this investigation, he related his own results to those reported in the literature.

He may have been a little surprised to discover that there were large areas of agreement between Western staff and his own respondents. All had degrees of confidence in self-, peer and student evaluation though they also cited similar sets of disadvantages and limitations. For example, they all questioned the validity of academic administrators' evaluations based on infrequent class observations and had little confidence in the formative value of evaluations by graduates or in evaluation based on students' examination results.

There were some differences between the groups, notably related to stress and threat which were frequently reported in the Western research and commonly associated with evaluations by department heads, but there were no indications that these were issues among Tim's respondents. He suggests that this may be due to what he describes as 'the supportive teaching culture of his polytechnic'.

He concludes:

A view held in common between staff of this research and those of others is that different people are better placed to make judgements about different aspects of teaching. For example, students can answer questions in the areas of pedagogical methods and lecturers' enthusiasm in teaching while peers can comment on the relevance and currency of teaching materials.

He acknowledges that neither his own results nor those reported in the literature suggest any 'best way' for carrying out teaching evaluations, but

> Understanding staff's attitudes and their confidence in the sources of evaluation can help academic administrators to lay out the options for an action plan for teaching evaluation. A judicious combination of teaching evaluation methods may well add up to much more than the sum of its parts.

That sounds sensible enough, though Timothy found frequent references in the literature to the unwillingness of academic staff to reach consensus about stated or intended purposes of SET and that is what he discovered from his own research. He found that though over 90 per cent of his respondents said they were willing to give student evaluations a place in the academic evaluation system in various ways, support fell significantly if they were intended to serve the purpose of identifying staff whose teaching performance needed improvement.

So, what conclusions can be drawn about the differences between Western academic staff and staff of the three participating departments in Tim's college? He was perhaps surprised that the similarities far outweighed the differences. His respondents had reached agreement about the most and least important characteristics of effective teaching, which coincided very closely with students' views, but reaching consensus about desirable *uses* of SET was quite another matter.

5.5

DISCUSSION

We asked Tim about his experiences of the five years of work as a part time student, including the way he planned his work, how he selected the topic and some of the methods and techniques he used. Like most of the other researchers whose work we have considered in this book, he had a full-time job and family responsibilities which made considerable demands on his time. Originally, he planned scheduled time slots for the research but found it impossible to keep to them. There were too many interruptions and demands on his time, everything took much longer and was more effort than he originally anticipated and getting restarted after an interruption was frustrating. Many of us have experienced similar frustrations. In the end he succeeded because he was committed, but it was never easy.

His topic gradually emerged from his supervisor's suggestions, from his work but also from his own developing interest in SET. He already had a Masters degree in auditing when he began the PhD and had become interested in the principles of quality auditing. His research was planned to be quantitative, but he needed to know what staff felt about SET, why some opposed it, what they thought about the characteristics of effective teaching and so much of his extensive preliminary work involved qualitative, face-to-face interviews, discussions and verbal feedback about questionnaire drafts.

> At each of the five draft stages of the questionnaire, I asked colleagues and members of the participating departments questions such as 'Why do you have least confidence in this characteristic of effective teaching?' One colleague said 'I'm not confident in our student evaluation at all.' When I asked why, he said it was because the wording of some of the questions wasn't right. He told me I was asking students the wrong things. We were able to talk about it and I was able to get more insight into why people thought as they did, why they had no confidence in student evaluation and why their perceptions were as they were. I got input from people at each stage of drafting and was able to refine and reorder the wording and content each time. They helped me a lot about wording. I knew the questionnaire had to be right because I couldn't afford to send it out and then think of something I should have asked so I had to spend this time on the drafts.

He was right, but the time spent certainly enabled him to produce a quality questionnaire. By the time he had gone through all five drafts, not one single item was redundant, the order of questions was good and the data produced enabled him to carry out the planned statistical tests.

He used SPSS 7.0, running under the operating system Windows 95. We wondered why he had used that system, whether he had considered any other and whether he had experienced any difficulties. He said he had used it because it was a system he knew and worked with as part of his job. It met all his requirements and there's no point in looking elsewhere if what is immediately available suits your purposes:

> Those of us who work in IT like to try out new things so I suppose my background and training helped me. It must be very difficult for people with an Arts background to identify the best software and the best system. I hadn't used all the SPSS programs before and I had some difficulty in interpreting the results of some of the unfamiliar software. I still had

to decide whether I should use this particular statistical approach or some other. Everybody does and it all depends on what you hope to get out of it.

We asked him what he felt were good outcomes from the research. Not surprisingly, he said he was really pleased he managed to complete the PhD and that it was successful. Well, who wouldn't have been pleased? It is a considerable achievement. He was also pleased to find so many staff were really keen about teaching and learning, wanted to learn more and do better. He said:

We're so tied down with teaching and admin work that it's hard to find time to do anything else but I learnt by being able to talk about our work. I was able to look seriously at the quality aspect of teaching, to listen to different voices, consider different performance indicators and different sources of feedback. We learnt from one another, talked about our problems and possible solutions.

Talking to students was helpful. They were quite explicit about what they did, what they liked and what they didn't. So, what I hope is that in some ways the research might have enhanced the culture of our teaching and learning.

We asked him then about any disappointments. He said he would have liked to generalize his findings to a wider population but there were sensitivities about releasing data and individual and institutional positions had to be respected. We understand those regrets, though we do have to say that a thesis which ran to almost 500 packed pages was already very large and to have extended it further might have made it impossible to manage.

He had some disappointments about researching at such a distance from the university where he was registered for the doctorate:

Working as a part-time external student was a lonely experience. I missed personal contact and opportunities to talk to other students. You can't tap into the rich university resources that are available to full-time students. You're not part of the culture, and you can't participate in the seminars. The facilities and the resources of the university don't benefit an external student. I missed all that.

He recognized that he had been fortunate in having a supportive supervisor. He was in regular email contact and had occasional telephone conversations with her. Short drafts of 10 or 12 pages were emailed but drafts of full chapters, some of which were very long, and particularly those which included graphics, had to be sent by post. They had agreed a 'turnround' schedule and she pretty well kept to that but, even so, there was a time gap of one or two weeks. He always felt anxious until he had received the reply and learnt whether he was going in the right direction. His anxiety is understandable but a consistent one- or two-week turnround is generally considered to be very good – significantly better than many supervisors have been able to achieve, even those whose office is no more than fifty yards away.

Even though library provision in Singapore is good, he still occasionally had to call on his supervisor for help in locating journals, which she always tried to do. When he was studying in London, he was able to go into one of the big academic libraries, particularly the University of London Institute of Education library, and could find almost everything there. He really missed that sort of opportunity.

We asked about writing up the thesis. Had he experienced any particular problems? We confidently expected him to mention the sort of difficulties that most researchers experience at this final stage but not a bit of it:

One issue is that English is not our first language. It is my third language so I think it took me longer to write than it would have been for people whose first language is English. That's the same for all overseas students. I think we make more errors so we need help with this. My supervisor helped me to clarify my thoughts and asked me things like 'Did you actually mean that?' because I might have been using inappropriate terms or language which might be interpreted in different ways. Even with terminology I had some difficulties.

For example, the use of 'course' and 'module', 'year of study' and 'grade' mean different things to different people.

Well Tim, perhaps we should go back to your thesis now and look for those 'errors' and 'inappropriate terms or language' because we didn't find any! I imagine many a researcher whose first, or even only, language is English would have been glad to have produced a thesis of this quality.

We asked what advice he would give to anyone taking on a doctoral study. He was quite clear about that:

I would say that they really have to calculate the costs. Not just the financial costs, though they can add up, but they have to understand the time needed and what they have to give up to be able to do it. They have to be really interested in the topic. If they aren't, it will be very hard to last out for four or five years. If they're researching as external students of an overseas university, they need to know they will have to work in silent mode.

I would tell them they have to be able to work through bad times but still keep going. I was really fed up with it at times but now that I look back I can see it was a good experience. I learnt a lot about research processes and had the opportunity to do an extensive amount of research which I never had the opportunity to do in my work. When I began to interpret the data, I knew I actually had the evidence to support what I was saying and that was a good feeling. Then it was really worthwhile.

FURTHER READING

Most statistics books will give definitions, examples and explanations of the statistics we discuss in this Part but, if you have no statistics background, some are heavy going. If you are planning to become involved in inferential statistics, you would be well advised first to consult your supervisor and whoever has responsibility for advising research students about data analysis. If at first you are told the university has no such person, persist. Ask around. Knock on doors if necessary. Ask other research students where they went for help. There might well be someone who knows everything about data analysis and statistical strategies and whose job it is to help research students. Some universities produce their own notes on the use of various statistical strategies so take advantage of what is provided. The following sources and the glossary will give definitions and examples but nothing beats face-to-face explanations.

Chi-square (X^2) and Spearman's rank of correlation coefficient (Spearman's rho)
All the following will provide brief accounts of the purpose of Spearman's rho (ρ) and provide good summaries of chi-square.

Bryman, A. and Cramer, D. (1994) (Revised edition) *Quantitative Data Analysis for Social Scientists*. London: Routledge.
Pages 159–64 provide a good account of the purpose and administration of chi-square. They discuss the statistical significance of the null hypothesis, significance levels, guidance about which SPSS commands to use and what tables will be provided.

Cramer, D. (1997) *Basic Statistics for Social Research.* London: Routledge. Pages 116–40 provide definitions and examples of chi-square for one or more unrelated samples, for one sample, for two unrelated samples and for three or more unrelated samples. As in all the examples given here, the explanations are a relatively hard read but worth the effort.

Greene, J. and D'Oliveira, M. (1982) *Learning to Use Statistical Tests in Psychology.* Buckingham: Open University Press. Pages 69–74 provide a particularly useful section, with examples, which includes When to use, Rationale, and Step-by-step instructions for calculating the value of chi-square. Spearman's rho is covered in pp. 138–41.

Rose, D. and Sullivan, O. (1996) *Introducing Data Analysis for Social Scientists,* 2nd edn. Buckingham: Open University Press. Pages 185–96 are useful. Assumptions about and limitations of inferential statistics are also discussed and multiple choice questions (and answers) are provided on p. 255.

Questionnaire design
Wilson, M. (1996) in Sapsford, R. and Jupp, V. (eds) *Data Collection and Analysis.* London: Sage. Pages 101–6, 'Asking questions', and pp. 106–7, 'Pilot studies', are well worth reading.

Reliability and validity
Rose and Sullivan (1996) discuss reliability on p. 246 and validity on p. 253. Clear and to the point.

Sapsford and Jupp (1996) Chapter 1, 'Validating evidence', provides a thorough account of the difference between reliability and validity.

Weighted averages
Clarke, G.M. and Cooke, D. (1992) *A Basic Course in Statistics,* 3rd edn. London: Edward Arnold. Pages 25–6 illustrate a system similar to Tim's in order to work out the average wage per person in a factory. Tim's calculation gave points to each of the five most important characteristics of effective teaching nominated by staff respondents. Weights assigned to each characteristic were 5 for the most important down to 1 for the fifth most important. The number of frequencies multiplied by the weights assigned in each category resulted in the total weighted score. The higher the WA score, the more important the characteristic as rated by the respondents.

CHECKLIST

1 Take care over the selection of the topic. It has to last you for the full period of the research.	Try to avoid being given a topic because someone thinks it should be investigated, unless you personally think it has enough in it to last out.
2 Make sure you define all your terms in the context of your study.	And that your readers (and particularly your examiners) know what you mean.
3 Read as much as you can before you commit yourself to the topic.	Look to the published research to discover what has already been done on your topic and how researchers planned their research.
3 As you read, begin to identify possible key issues and groupings.	Don't ever end up with piles of paper and rough notes thrown into a drawer. The process of data reducing begins as soon as you start to read but take care over selectivity and potential biasing factors.
4 Take care also over claiming reliability and validity.	Make sure you understand the meaning and requirements for each.
5 Decide on and define your population.	And don't assume you will automatically have access to any individual, group, materials or records. Make formal requests for access and make sure the recipients understand fully what you are asking for.

6 Always carry out well-managed pilot studies.	As we have repeatedly said, they are essential, not an option.
7 One-shot questionnaires and/or other data-collecting instruments are likely to be a disaster.	Remember the number of drafts Timothy required, the number of people he consulted, the times he had to reword, eliminate or add? That's what's required or the analysis will be a nightmare.
8 If you plan to analyse data by computer, make sure you know which software to use (and why), how to use it and what the printouts mean.	But first be sure exactly what you need to know before you even think about which programs to use. If you are advised that certain statistical tests will give you the results you need, be sure you understand the assumptions they make, what they do and what they are testing. If you have doubts or don't understand, ASK SOMEONE WHO KNOWS.
9 Write up as much as you can as you go along.	Better to have badly written drafts and notes but not nearly as bad as having to face blank pages.
10 If you've managed to keep friends during the course of the research, ask them if they will read drafts, and don't take offence if they criticize or point out errors. That's what you want, not compliments which just might indicate they have read them in two minutes flat.	Be nice to them. They will be doing you a favour and researchers need all the help they can get.

POSTSCRIPT

LEARNING FROM RESEARCH

If ever our five researchers were to meet one day and the conversation happened to turn to research in general, and to their experiences in particular, they would find they had faced many similar but also many different high and low points at various stages of their MEd or PhD. During the course of their voyages of discovery, they learnt a great deal. All made some mistakes but they learnt from them and it's unlikely they will ever make the same ones again. We say 'unlikely' because we've never known any researchers who can really claim *never* to have made the same mistakes twice. These things happen. We all say they will never happen again and, at the time, we mean it.

Only Jan was researching full-time, and it would have been very difficult to have undertaken her ethnographic topic as a part-timer. The other four were studying part-time, had full-time jobs and were studying at a distance. Fortunately, they all had experienced and supportive supervisors. Helen was only 50 or so miles away from her supervisor but Gilbert, Cher Ping and Tim were on the other side of the world from where they were registered for their degree. With e-mail, it may seem immaterial where students are based. All five were able to draw on the resources of their own university, local library or polytechnic but, as Tim rather sadly remembers, it's not the same as being there. You aren't part of the culture of the university, don't have access to its library, other facilities, face-to-face contact with research supervisors and seminars. Gilbert agreed. He too would have liked closer contact with his university and with fellow students. We are all different though and Cher Ping was content to work alone. He was a very independent worker and preferred to go at his own pace in his own time and without being bothered too much by his supervisor. As he said, working at a distance is OK 'as long as you can learn on your own', though even he would have liked more contact with fellow research students.

All experienced bad patches from time to time when things just weren't going right. At one point, Helen remembers asking herself why she was doing the MEd. Why was she allowing it to ruin her life? She recalls that she had to remind herself that she had never been a quitter. She certainly wasn't, nor were any of the others.

Originally, Tim planned to allocate regular time slots to his research, but interruptions and the demands of home and work made it impossible for him to keep to such a regular pattern. He just did the best he could to keep up to date because he knew that if he fell seriously behind he might not be able to catch up.

In some of the very bad days, Gilbert experienced what he called 'giving up syndrome'. At times, the demands of his job made it necessary to put the research on hold and then it was very difficult to get started again. No doubt many of you have had similar experiences. He was helped by the fact that he was really interested in his topic, in sorting out the methodology and in analysing the data. It was that strong interest which kept him going and when his data began to produce interesting findings, then suddenly it was 'sunshine days all the way', as it was for all of them.

Even Jan, who was by far the most experienced researcher, recalled difficult times when she was in something of a fog, until what she described as 'the enlightenment'. Do you recall that the fog began to lift in one particular meeting when suddenly all the pieces of her complex picture came together?

Although they were all so successful, every one of them felt they could have done better in different ways. A better system of indexing and cross-referencing so that it would have been easier to locate references immediately; better skill in computer use and in the use of statistical packages; better interviewing skills and, given time, better quality writing. On and on they went. They were very thorough and open about mentioning their weak points but less so about what they did well. They had no wish to be boastful! As you will have seen in the views they expressed about their research experience in the Discussion chapters of each of the five accounts, they all learnt a great deal about so many things including literature searching, writing their review of the literature, and about the need to read widely before finally deciding on the precise focus of their investigations. They learnt, to their cost in one or two cases, that failing to carry out well-structured pilot studies can cause much grief later on in the investigation. They knew, or learnt quickly, that all references have to be fully noted and that the back of old envelopes or shopping lists are not good places on which to write notes. They learnt that if notes of what has been read are not made during or immediately after the reading, it may be impossible to recall what the books or articles were about some time later. We all think we shall remember, but the odds are that we shan't.

Could they have got more out of their data? Yes. In most cases their preparation was sufficiently thorough, the purpose of their studies sufficiently clear and their data-collecting instruments sufficiently well designed and, in most cases, piloted to have enabled them to do more, but more would have been too much. Most discovered they needed to establish boundaries to their research and by and large they kept to them. That is not only good sense but essential because otherwise the dissertations and theses would never have been submitted. There is always more that can be explored.

It is our view that the quality of their preparation was the key to their successful research and their ability to extract as much as they needed from their data. Even though three of the five researchers were statistically competent, no amount of statistical wizardry would have saved them if they had spent insufficient time on planning and preparation. There are no short cuts in research and no quick fixes and they came to know that. Perhaps we should also add that they were formidably hard workers, were absolutely determined to succeed and, even in the bad days, nothing would have made them give up. These qualities all help.

GLOSSARY

Averages: (see *central tendency measures of*)

Bias: Dictionary definitions of 'bias' vary but generally centre on the notion of distortion of judgement, prejudiced outlook, unfair influence. They sound reasonable enough but there can be problems over interpretation because one person's 'fair and unbiased point of view' may well be judged to be 'prejudice' by another. In Part 4 of the book, we asked whether there were any signs of bias in Jan's review of the literature. Had she selected only those items which supported her point of view? Had she used any inappropriate language which might have indicated strength of feeling in one direction? She recalls that it was her constant questioning of practice and her critical attitude towards the interpretation of data which helped her to recognize signs of bias. She was personally involved in her selected area of research and knew she had to consider the extent to which her value judgements might influence the way she interpreted research findings and her own data.

In Part 5, you will recall that Tim was concerned about the lack of an agreed definition of 'bias' in the literature. He found that writers rarely declared their assumptions and though many research reports claimed steps had been taken to eliminate bias, there appeared to be no agreement about what it actually was. One definition was that 'it is a circumstance that unduly influences teachers' ratings'. Sounds reasonable, but he found that was difficult to test. Another was that 'student ratings are biased to the extent that they are influenced by variables that are unrelated to teaching effectiveness'. That could well be so, but which variables? Miles and Huberman, writing about qualititative research, warn:

> We have moments of illumination. Things 'come together'. The problem is that we could be wrong. A near-library of research evidence shows that people (researchers included) habitually tend to *overweight* facts they believe in or depend on, to *ignore or forget* data not going in the direction of their reasoning and to *'see' confirming instances* far more easily than disconfirming instances (Nisbett and Ross 1980). We do this by differentially weighting information, and by looking at part of the data, not all of them.
> (Miles and Huberman 1994: 253–4, original emphasis)

When all the pieces of Jan's research jigsaw came together (what she described as 'the process of enlightenment') and she was able to see the full picture, she still had to ask herself whether she had 'overweighted' the facts because of her personal beliefs. She knew the dangers and that was why she placed so much emphasis on reflection on practice and on triangulation.

Central tendency (measures of): There are three types of average (more properly known as measures of central tendency), namely the *mean, median and mode,* each of which serves a different purpose. The *mean* is simple to calculate. To find the mean of nine values, add them up and then divide by nine. Let's say our nine values are 2, 3, 3, 4, 62, 4, 5, 5, 5. The sum of these values is 93, which divided by 9 produces a mean of 10.3. The *median* considers the order of the data. Look at our nine values again. There's an extreme value among the nine which has distorted the mean and so the *median* may give a better sense of the 'centre' of the data. Put the numbers into ascending order, which gives us 2, 3, 3, 4, 4, 5, 5, 5, 62. The median is the middle value, which is 4 and that gives an altogether more realistic picture than the mean for these nine numbers.

The *mode*, which is not often used in small studies, relates to the most frequently occurring value. In our case, this is obviously 5.

Each of these measures of central tendency has different uses and, as always, it all depends what you need to know and why. If we were more interested in the spread or dispersion of the data rather than the mean, we should need to calculate the *standard deviation (SD)*. The mean is used as the measure of central tendency, but the SD is always used as the measure of dispersion. It reflects the degree to which the values differ from the mean (see standard deviation later in the glossary).

(*See also* Bell 1999: 177–80; Bryman and Cramer (1994: 82–94); Denscombe 1998: 193–8.)

Chi-square (χ^2) is a test of statistical significance which allows us to assess whether there is a *significant* relationship between two variables or whether there is no apparent relationship which could reasonably have arisen by chance. The starting point is always the *null hypothesis*. Let's say a school canteen was interested to know whether, all other things being equal, changing the shape of its vegetable samosas would influence pupils' lunchtime selection. A member of staff of the school, who had recently carried out chi-square tests as part of a postgraduate research study, volunteered to carry out a formal investigation into the viability of changing the shapes of samosas. Her first step was to establish a null hypothesis which stated that '*the shape of samosas has no effect on sales*' and she then set about the task of setting up an experiment which would enable the null hypothesis to be accepted or rejected. Samosas were cooked in three different shapes, square, round and triangular. Sales figures for the first 120 samosas sold were examined and a cross-tabulation (also known as a contingency table) of actual and expected sales produced. If the null hypothesis were to be accepted (that is, the shape of samosas has no effect on sales), then the expected number of sales would be 40 of each shape. However, in our imaginary example, there were clear differences, as is illustrated in the following table.

	Square	Round	Triangular
Actual (observed) purchases	36	20	64
Expected purchases	40	40	40

There will always be some differences between the observed and the expected purchases, but the question for the school was *how* different? The cross-tabulation provided quite interesting information but the school needed to know whether these findings were *significant*.

Before any further tests could be carried out the **significance** **(probability)** level had to be set, and in this experiment the teacher–researcher set the probability at the 0.01 level ($p = 0.01$) (that is, only one time in a hundred would the result have been likely to occur by chance). Once all the initial preparation was done the stage was reached when chi-square could be calculated.

It's quite possible to calculate chi-square manually for small numbers, but much easier (and, unless you're very careful, more accurate) by computer, particularly for a large amount of data. As long as your data from the contingency table are fed into the computer accurately and instructions given for the chi-square statistic to be carried out, the job will be done for you, the chi-square statistic produced and the p value indicated.

There's a lot more to chi-square than we have indicated here and there are many good books on the market which will give you the full picture, but as we have said many times throughout the book, the important part of any research is that we should understand *what* we need to know and *why* before we begin to consider which tests will be appropriate. And before you launch into complex statistics, check with your supervisor (and whoever is responsible for advising research students in your institution) that chi-square is the statistic you need for your purposes.

(*See* Bryman and Cramer 1994: 159–64; Cohen and Holliday 1996: 126–7; Punch 1998: 115–16, 132–5; and Rose and Sullivan 1996: 185–90, all of whom provide information about calculating chi-square and guidance about SPSS computation of chi-square values. Greene and D'Oliveria 1982: 69–73 discuss the rationale for the chi-square test and give step-by-step instructions for calculating the value of chi-square).

Coding and the code book/coding key: All data have to be classified or categorized in some way for them to have any meaning. In quantitative research where raw data are to be analysed by computer, variables have to be allocated a number (a code) so that the computer is able to understand our instructions. But coding is not restricted to quantitative data, because order has to be produced from qualitative *and* from quantitative data. Coding *is* analysis – or at any rate is the foundation on which analysis can be made. It is the grouping or categorizing of responses to any data-collecting instrument, in numbers, words or phrases. Miles and Huberman (1994: 56) and Punch (1998: 204) describe codes as 'tags', 'labels' or 'names' which enable researchers to differentiate and combine data – and that process starts early and continues throughout the entire period of the research.

You can allocate any numbers you like to codes. They are merely labelling devices but, as you can imagine, it's rather important to keep a complete record of which numbers you have allocated to which item – and every item on your data-collecting instrument must be included. You can call that record what you like – code book, data key, coding key. The title isn't important but the fact that you have that record is.

(*See* Rose and Sullivan 1996: 41–2, who give brief but very useful and clear guidance about the purpose of code books and Oppenheim 1992: 261–78 who provides a thorough account of coding under the headings of 'Assembling the code book'; 'The data base'; 'Serial case numbering'; 'Coding frames'; 'The coding process'; and 'Problems of coding reliability'.)

(Punch (1998: 204–21) and Miles and Huberman (1994: 55–72 and 249–50) both provide excellent discussion of coding for qualitative analysis.)

(*See also* Helen's study in Part 1, p. 22 of the book which considers codes and coding and requirements for preparing data for the computer.)

Concepts are abstractions and concepts can't actually be seen, observed or measured. 'Satisfaction', 'perception' and 'class' are concepts and if we wish to measure, for example, students' satisfaction with their course, we have to identify indicators. What do we observe, read or are told which indicates students' satisfaction? Rose and Sullivan (1996: 12–13) suggest that indicators of 'class' might include occupation and employment status, which would be one step from the concept 'class' to the measurable variables of occupation and unemployment status.

(*See* Dixon *et al.* 1987: 50–63 which deal with concepts and variables. They also provide clear examples of ways in which concepts can be operationalized. This book is rather old now, but none the worse for that and if you can find a copy in your library, it's worth consulting.)

(*See also* Gilbert's study in Part 2, p. 48 of the book.)

Conceptual frameworks are theoretical and exploratory devices which 'explain, either graphically or in narrative form, the main things to be studied – the key factors, constructs or variables and the presumed relationships among them' (Miles and Huberman 1994: 18). They recommend working with diagrams rather than with words and getting the entire framework on to a single page to enable researchers 'to map likely relationships, to divide variables that are conceptually or functionally distinct, and to work with all of the information at once' (p. 22).

In Part 2, Figure 1, p. 47 of the book, Gilbert began the first stage in establishing his conceptual framework when he produced the first thoughts flow chart of factors influencing students' level of satisfaction with their Diploma in Nursing programme. 'Level of satisfaction with Diploma in Nursing programme' was his core issue, with related factors (what Miles and Huberman call 'bins') contributing to the core. It was a start, but there was much more work to be done before his framework was clear. He had to be able to understand the relationship between one bin and another, what was in each *and* what methods of data collecting would be needed in order to complete the picture of how the research would proceed. Not a task to be completed in an odd few minutes here and there, but a much longer procedure which changed many times before he was satisfied that all likely possibilities had been considered.

Content validity 'seeks to establish that the items or questions are a well-balanced sample of the content domain to be measured' (Oppenheim 1992: 162). In Part 5 of the book, Tim made a particular point of asking his pilot group members to comment on the content validity of his questionnaire items in order to be sure they adequately covered the content or area of concern being considered. In other words, had he omitted any essential aspects which related to the questionnaire topic/s? And was due attention given to the balance of the selected topics?

Control group: (see experimental research).

Correlation (r): Cross-tabulations merely show the numbers giving one answer (or a grouped answer) for one item against those of another but they give no idea of the strength of association or relationship between the variables. **Correlation coefficients** enable degrees of association, if any, to be established. The coefficient always falls between +1.00 (perfect correspondence between the two variables, which would be very unlikely) and –1.00 (equally unlikely). It's usual to omit the plus sign and so a correlation of 0.8 or more would indicate a strong positive correlation whereas a value of – 0.3 or less would indicate a weak negative correlation. Most textbooks provide examples of how to calculate 'r'.

(*See* Greene and D'Oliveira 1982: Chapter 9, pp. 132–44; Cohen and Manion 1994: 126–45. *See also* Gilbert's use of correlation coefficients in Part 2, p. 66.)

Correlation and causation: Correlation and causation are not the same thing. In the social sciences, it's difficult if not impossible to design research in such a way as to eliminate every possible contaminating factor, so take great care in assuming that one variable actually causes another. Oppenheim (1992: 15) reminds us about Sir Francis Galton's investigation into the 'objective efficacy of prayer'. He wanted to find out, for reasons which were no doubt of great importance to him at the time, whether clergymen lived longer than members of other professions. His data showed a small association between praying and longevity but Oppenheim cautions us that even if Galton's data had shown a very large difference in the average age attained by clergy compared with other professions, there just might be other factors which had a greater influence on longevity than prayer. For example, he writes that

> it might be that in those days the clergy attracted exceptionally healthy recruits with a predisposition to longevity. Or the results might be explained by another, more current, association; clergymen might be sustained into old age by exceptionally supportive wives!
>
> (Oppenheim 1992: 15)

(*See* Bryman and Cramer 1994: 8–16 who give clear explanations of the dangers of assuming that one variable causes another. They discuss 'Causality and research design'; 'Establishing causality'; 'Causality and experimental design'; 'Survey design and causality'. Oppenheim's 1992: 13–18 discussion of problems associated with cause and effect are also well worth reading.)

Cross-tabulation: Cross-tabulations consist of tables which have a row of variables on the horizontal axis and other variables down the vertical axis which show frequencies, though not relationships, between two or more variables. A simple illustration of a cross-tabulation would be on the following lines:

Table xyz Numbers of absences in experimental and control groups

	Experimental group	*Control group*	*Total*
Number of times absent	3	22	25
Number of times present	22	32	54
Total	25	54	79

There are two variables in this example, namely group (experimental and control) and attendance (absent or present). The columns represent the groups and the rows represent absence or attendance. Cross-tabulations are descriptive statistics and summarize data. That's all right as far as it goes, but if information were required about the relationship between the variables, then more complex statistics would be required, such as correlation coefficients.

Dependent and independent variables: A variable is termed *independent* if it is considered to have some effect on a *dependent* variable. For example, if we hypothesize that income is affected by gender, then income would be the dependent variable and gender the independent variable. Nobody would seriously consider that gender depended on income, would they?

In Cher Ping's experimental study in Part 3, p. 93 of the book, you may recall that he was very careful to check that the experimental and control groups shared similar characteristics. He took care to ensure both followed the same syllabus and that methods of assessment were the same. This enabled him to have some confidence that the improved performance of the experimental group was *dependent* on the CBL programme. So the CBL programme was the *independent variable* and students' examination results were the *dependent variable*.

(*See* Soloman and Winch 1994: 66 and Calder 1996: 228–9. See also Part 3, p. 93 of Cher Ping's experimental study.)

Descriptive statistics are used to summarize, describe and present pictures of data. They include frequencies, frequency and percentage distributions, cross-tabulations, averages (mean, median and mode) and are often presented in the form of charts or tables.

Dialectic: In Part 4, p. 151, Jan wrote that 'it was not possible to avoid the dialectic between the observed and the interpreted worlds'. Dictionary definitions of 'dialectic' generally centre around the principle of testing the truth of an opinion or theory by logical discussion. Jan frequently had to face challenges to her own opinions, beliefs and theories, particularly when what she observed was at odds with some of the participants' firmly held beliefs about the culture of compulsory education. Her discussions with participants about the various 'truths' must have been important steps in reaching understanding of the issues she was exploring.

Dichotomous variables are variables which can only be classified into two categories. For example, responses to questions about gender can only be classified into male or female and so 'gender' is a dichotomous variable.

Ethics in research: Most institutions and professional organisations which are involved in research will have codes of conduct to which researchers must conform. However, regardless of whether there are codes, principles, guidelines or whatever, all researchers will do well to remember Sapsford and Abbott's (1996: 318–19) insistence that a first principle of research ethics is that the subjects of the research should not be *harmed* by it. Obvious? Well yes. It should be, but they remind us that some startling breaches of research ethics have been reported in the literature over a period of time.

Throughout the book, you will know that we have urged researchers to be precise in defining their role, to be clear about what they mean by anonymity and confidentiality and to make sure their participants interpret their definitions in the same way.

(*See also* Hart and Bond 1995: 199; Blaxter *et al.* 1996: 146; Cohen and Manion 1994: 347–84; and Miles and Huberman 1994: 288–97; Bell 1999: 38–47, 141–2, 153.)

Ethnographic research: There are a good many definitions of ethnography and ethnographic research and not all ethnographic researchers agree about what it is. We'll give just two definitions, the first given by Jan in Part 4 of the book. She described ethnographic research as 'a search for meaning, the development of an understanding of how a culture works, whether it's of an institution, a classroom or the culture of a phenomenon', and that simple definition seems to us to get to the heart of this approach. Brewer (2000: 10) takes the definition further when he describes ethnography as 'the study of people in naturally occurring settings or "fields" by means of methods which capture their social meanings'. It involves researchers in participating directly 'in order to collect data in a systematic manner but without meaning being imposed on them externally'.

(*See also* Denscombe 1998: Chapter 5 and Punch 1998: 157–62.)

Experimental research: The principle of experimental research is that if two identical groups are selected, one of which (the experimental group) is given special treatment and the other (the control group) is not, then any differences between the two groups at the end of the experimental period may be attributed to the difference in treatment (Bell 1999: 15). Of course, it's not quite as simple as that, as you will know from Cher Ping's account of the steps he took to establish groups which shared similar demographic and aptitude characteristics and were following the same course with the same assessment criteria. The only difference was that the experimental group followed the computer-based learning programme and the control group followed the usual college remedial programme.

(*See* Cher Ping's experimental study in Part 3 of the book *and also* Chapter 12 of Cohen *et al.* 2000, and Chapter 2 of Greene, J. and D'Oliveira, M. 1982).

Frequencies are the numbers of items in each specified category, such as the number of women respondents in a study and the number of men, or the number of students' unauthorized absences from school. It might be interesting, or even worrying, to know that there were

100 unauthorized absences in Class 3 during the summer term, but that figure gives no idea of the length of the absences and so a **grouped frequency distribution** table or chart might be far more revealing. For example, in a class of 30, we might group numbers in order to see the distribution of absences more clearly. Absolute numbers or percentages can be used.

Days absent	Frequencies
0–2	2
3–5	10
6–8	4
9–11	3
12–14	3
15+	8

Hypotheses are statements about possible relationship between variables. They are 'hunches, tentative propositions which are subject to verification through subsequent investigation' (Verma and Beard 1981: 184), and a 'speculative adventure, an imaginative preconception of *what might be true*' (Medawar 1972: 22). They serve as a guide to researchers as to how the research should proceed. If our experience leads us to believe that students who eat breakfast every morning do better in examinations than those who do not, that might be the basis for our hypothesis. This hunch would be difficult to test as it stands and we should need to be far more precise about which students are included (all the students in the world, in the University of Hardtimes, Class 2 in a primary school?) and in which conditions or context (over a 20-year period, over one school year, end-of-week tests, degree finals?). On and on until all the bugs have been eliminated and the researchers are left with what is likely to be a testable hypothesis.

There is some concern about using a hypothesis in mainly descriptive studies when no statistical testing is to take place (Moser and Kalton 1971: 4 and Punch 1998: 40–1). It is suggested that the objectives of the study and/or the development of research questions would serve the purpose perfectly well and we agree with this point of view.

(*See also null hypothesis.*)

Indicators: An indicator is a variable which can be counted or measured. In Part 2, Gilbert set out to measure students' satisfaction with their

Diploma in Nursing course. 'Satisfaction' is an abstraction, a mental construct which can't be seen, observed or measured and so he had to think of ways in which students might provide *indications* of satisfaction with the course. In order to do that, he turned his unobservable concepts into variables and then into indicators which enabled him to measure degrees of satisfaction.

In hotel rooms, there are frequently questionnaires asking clients whether they were satisfied with the hotel's services and tables and charts are regularly produced indicating that 99 per cent of clients were very satisfied with the hotel's services. In research, we can't indulge in this degree of fudging because we need to clarify our thoughts about what we mean by satisfaction before we can identify appropriate measurable variables. Are we referring to satisfaction with our room? If so, in which ways? Cleanliness? Sheets? Time taken to repair faults? Lighting? Ventilation? Location (on top of the kitchen fan, smell from the dustbins)? Or wonderful views of the hills, newly refurbished room, quality furnishing? Repairs dealt with in five minutes – or never? The process of breaking down 'satisfaction' continues until we have identifiable *and measurable* variables. Which instruments would be appropriate? Observation? Time sheets? Checklists? Interviews? Think about it. The concept 'satisfaction' means nothing until the indicators of satisfaction are specified.

(*See* Dixon *et al.* 1987. Chapter 5, pp. 64–103 ('Finding a variable's measurements') is well worth reading. Many useful examples are given, including the procedures involved in the relationship between concepts, variables and measuring instruments.)

Inferential statistics: Descriptive statistical methods are able to provide 'pictures' of a group under investigation but inferential statistics have a quite different purpose. They may involve the use of descriptive statistics but their prime aim is to draw inferences from the data with regard to a theory, model or body of knowledge (Goulding 1987: 103). They allow the researcher to demonstrate the probability that the results derived from a sample are likely to be found in the population from which the sample was taken, but as Bryman and Cramer warn (1994: 5), only if a random sample has been selected.

(*See* Cher Ping's work in relation to his hypothesis testing and t-tests in Part 3 of the book.)

Likert scales are devices to discover strength of feeling or attitude towards a given statement or series of statements. In Part 2, Gilbert used a Likert scale which asked respondents to indicate their agreement or disagreement with the following statement:

If the present educational criteria for the diploma in nursing programme are lowered, more people will be encouraged to take up nursing as a course of study:

Very strongly disagree	Strongly disagree	Disagree	Agree	Strongly agree	Very strongly agree
1	2	3	4	5	6

The implication here is that the higher the category chosen, the greater the strength of agreement but care has to be taken not to read too much in these scales. They indicate order, but nothing else, and we cannot assume that the differences between each number are the same.

Mean, median and mode: (see central tendency).

Measurement: In quantitative investigations, researchers invariably need to consider ways in which data can be classified and measured and which allow us to differentiate between one category and another. Concepts such as 'satisfaction' and 'self-esteem' are mental constructs. We can't actually see them and so have to consider how they can be expressed in ways which allow us to measure them. What can we actually observe which allows us to believe students are satisfied with their course and what behaviour indicates to us that an individual is suffering from low self-esteem? In Part 2, p. 48 of the book, Gilbert devised ways of testing students' satisfaction with their Diploma in Nursing by identifying indicators of satisfaction and linking his concepts to indicators. In this way, he was able to allocate numbers to his data in such a way as to demonstrate difference between categories.

Nominal (or categorical) scales are numbers (codes) which serve to identify categories into which items are to be classified. The codes have no numerical value, are completely arbitrary and are merely labelling devices. In Part 1, p. 23, Helen coded 'female' as 1 and 'male' as 2. She could have allocated any numbers.

Null hypothesis: The wording of the null hypothesis has to be precise, expressed in ways which enable it to be tested and, on the basis of the results of the tests, accepted or rejected.

In Part 3, p. 97, you may remember that in his experimental study into the effectiveness of computer-based learning, Cher Ping's null hypothesis (H_0) stated that in terms of mid-year and final grade scores, 'There is no significant difference between students in the experimental and the control group.' He was into the area of inferential statistics and tests of significance and the null hypothesis was the starting point for his tests.

Researchers start from the position that there is no significant difference 'until they can be persuaded otherwise by a statistical test which tells them that there is a very strong likelihood that any variation found between the two sets of data were the result of something other than pure chance' (Denscombe 1998: 201).

Most statistics books will have sections on hypothesis testing and the role of the null hypothesis, but also *see* Cohen and Manion 1994: 18–19, Denscombe 1998: 200–5 and Punch 1998: 39–41. (*See also chi-square* and *t-tests.*)

Ordinal scales are used to indicate rank order. In Tim's survey of teaching effectiveness in Part 5 of the book, he asked his questionnaire respondents to place what they considered to be the five most important characteristics of effective teaching in rank order, number 1 being the most important. Likert scales provide an example of the use of rank order.

(*See also Ranking,* Gilbert's use of Likert scales in Part 2, p. 54 of the book, and Tim's rank order questionnaire in Part 4, p. 203.)

Probability (or confidence) levels: In his experimental study, Cher Ping had to decide on the probability (p) level before he could carry out his t-tests. The level chosen is arbitrary but, by convention, most p levels will be likely to be set at around five times in a hundred ($p = 0.05$) or once in a hundred ($p = 0.01$). He chose the demanding once-in-a-hundred probability, perhaps because that reflected his computer-based learning (CBL) experience or because of his understanding of the published research relating to CBL.

Reflexivity is the process of thought and review which involves researchers in questioning their understanding and interpretation of their data and the extent to which their own beliefs and values may have influenced that understanding. Jan, in Part 4 of the book, found she had to stand back from her research and to remove it from the level of fieldwork, data collection and analysis to the level of abstractions. This process was important because it forced her to confront the possibility of biased interpretations and to question whether her own values and beliefs conflicted with the evidence of previous research. (*See also dialectic.*)

Reliability is the extent to which a test or procedure produces similar results under similar conditions and on different occasions. For example, if a respondent gives one answer to a questionnaire item one day but a different one on another, it might be suggested that the item was unreliable – though of course, there is also the possibility that the respondent might equally be unreliable.

Spearman's rank order coefficient (Spearman's rho): Spearman's rho is a statistical test which 'measures the amount and significance of a *correlation* between people's scores on two variables' (Green and D'Oliveira 1982: 138). It is used when ordinal data are involved. Tim selected this as one of several tests intended to discover the effect of respondents' background variables on their perceptions of the most important characteristics of effective teaching. His first task was to construct a series of null hypotheses, which stated:

There is no significant difference at the 0.05 level among the perceptions of the respondents with reference to the top five perceived characteristics based on their Department (H1), Gender (H2), Age (H3) etc.

H1 (department) was constructed in order to identify whether staff of the departments included in the study differed in their perceptions of the most important characteristics of effective teaching. A Spearman's rho of +1 would indicate perfect agreement between the two sets of data and the rho of –1 would indicate perfect disagreement, both of which would be very rare. Just to give one example, Tim's calculations revealed, among other things, that Department A correlated with Department C gave a rho of 0.843 (the + sign is not usually included in positive correlations). This high positive value enabled him to suggest that there was no significant difference at the 0.05 level between these two departments – and so the null hypothesis was accepted. Remember that correlation coefficients are about probability, not proof.

(*See* Tim's account in Part 5, p. 209 and the *chi-square, correlation, hypotheses* and *probability* sections elsewhere in the glossary.)

Standard deviation (SD): The standard deviation is a measure of the spread within a set of data. It's easy to calculate, even on inexpensive calculators (though you may need to look at the instruction booklet to see how to do it), and if you are using a computer the SD will often be automatically produced in association with the mean. Let's look at two sets of numbers, which are:

| Group A: | 48 | 49 | 50 | 51 | 52 |
| Group B: | 40 | 45 | 50 | 55 | 60 |

If you add the numbers for each group and divide by 5, you will see that the mean is 50 in each case, but the spread of scores in Group B is much wider than Group A. The SD will give information about the extent of the spread which in this example is 1.4 (very little spread) for Group A but 7.1 (a much wider spread) for Group B.

Most, probably all, statistics books will provide examples of the purpose and methods of calculating standard deviations if you need more detailed information.

Theory: Theory can be, and frequently is, defined in a good many ways. It can be taken to be the current state of knowledge about the topic being studied, which is likely to be derived from existing published research. It can be 'a set of interrelated abstract propositions about human affairs and the social world that explain their regularities and properties' (Brewer 2000: 192), or it can be 'a proposition about the relationship between things' (Denscombe 1998: 192).

Distinctions are made between what Wolcott (1992) describes as *theory first* or *theory after*. Punch clarifies these terms as follows:

> In theory-first research, we start with a theory, deduce hypo-theses from it, and design a study to test these hypotheses. This is theory verification. In theory-after research, we do not start with a theory. Instead, the aim is to end up with a theory, developed systematically from the data we have collected. This is theory generation.
>
> (Punch 1998: 16)

If you look back to the five investigations we have discussed in the book, you will see that Helen, Gilbert, Cher Ping and Tim adopted the theory-first approach by scouring the published research relating to their topic. Jan also spent a great deal of time identifying the relevant issues before she moved into the data-collecting stage of her research but she was eventually able to establish the theory relating to the culture of compulsory education in her specified educational and geographical research area (theory after).

Triangulation: Cohen and Manion (1994: 233) define triangulation as 'the use of two or more methods of data collection in the study of human behaviour'. It involves cross-checking of evidence, obtaining data from more than one respondent, comparing and contrasting one account with others, which is what Jan did in her ethnographic study.

t-tests: If you refer back to Part 3, you will see that one of the tasks Cher Ping set himself was to discover the degree of change from mid-year to final grades for his experimental and control group. He selected t-tests, which are statistical tests of significance, because he wished to find out whether the difference between the two groups was sufficiently large to suggest that it was unlikely to have been due to chance. He started by constructing a null hypothesis (H_0) which stated that 'There is no significant difference between the mean of mid-year and final grade levels of students in the experimental and control groups.' He considered that if the mean of the grade levels of the experimental group proved to be higher than that of the control group, he might perhaps be able to infer that his experimental (computer-based learning) programme produced the difference. But 'perhaps' was not good enough. He needed to discover whether the difference between the two means could reasonably have arisen by chance or whether it was *significantly* higher – and that involved decisions about *probability (significance) levels*.

The level selected is arbitrary, though by convention it is generally set at around five times in a hundred ($p = 0.05$) or once in a hundred ($p = 0.01$). Cher Ping set the level at 0.01 as the criterion for significance/non-significance which is the level of probability that only once in a hundred times would the results have arisen by chance. So, the procedures were that he had:

1 decided exactly what he wished to find out for a sample of his size (11 in the control group and 9 in the experimental group);
2 decided which statistical test would be likely to produce the necessary answers;
3 selected t-tests;
4 devised a null hypothesis;
5 set the probability level of 0.01;
6 calculated the means and standard deviations of the two grade scores.

(Based on Calder 1996: 247)

His next step was to compute the t-test statistic and then to decide whether to accept or reject the null hypothesis. The calculations are quite complex to carry out manually but, as in the case of chi-square, if you make use of an appropriate computer statistical package, the calculation of the t-statistic will be done for you and the probability level indicated which will help you to accept or reject your null hypotheses. Hurrah for computers!

If you're determined to calculate the t-statistic manually, most statistics books will give the formulae and procedures for carrying out the tests, but whether you are calculating manually or by computer, the crunch comes, as always, in interpreting the results, deciding what they mean and what can legitimately be claimed from them. Unless you are a competent statistician, you will need to ask for advice from someone who is, before you jump to the sort of conclusions which may invalidate your research. If you really do wish to carry out the calculations manually, the following books will provide examples and instructions for calculating the t-statistic.

(*See* Greene and D'Oliveira 1982: 89–98; Cramer 1997: 174–89; Bryman and Cramer 199: 134–49 and Calder 1996: 244–53. *See also chi-square, hypothesis* and *null hypothesis*.)

Validity: The usual definition of validity is that it tells us whether an item or instrument measures or describes what it is supposed to measure or describe but this is rather vague and leaves many questions unanswered.

Sapsford and Jupp (1996: 1) give a more precise definition. They take 'validity' to mean 'the design of research to provide credible conclusions; whether the evidence which the research offers can bear the weight of the interpretation that is put on it'. They argue that what has to be established is

[whether data] *do* measure or characterize what the authors claim, and that the interpretations *do* follow from them. The structure of a piece of research determines the conclusions that can be drawn from it and, most importantly, the conclusions that *should not* be drawn from it.

(Sapsford and Jupp 1996: 1, original emphasis)

(*See* Oppenheim 1992: 147–9 and 160–3; Sapsford and Jupp 1996: 1–23; Denscombe 1998: 213–14; Bell 1999: 103–4; Brewer 2000: 46–50.)

Variables: Variables are measurable characteristics or attributes. They are said to be *discrete* if they take whole number values, for example, the size of each section of a library where only whole numbers of books would be counted or numbers of children in a family. A variable which can take any value is *continuous*. For example, age would be a continuous variable though we have to be clear about what we mean by age. Do we mean the approximate or the exact age of the respondent? Or do we say something like 'age on the 25 March' – or something else? Decisions have to be made before any data-collecting instruments are distributed. How precise do we want to be? Too much detail clogs up the research; too little may not be helpful.

REFERENCES

Baker, S. (1999) Finding and searching information sources, in J. Bell, *Doing Your Research Project: A Guide for First-time Researchers in Education and Social science*. Buckingham: Open University Press.

Bassey, M. (1981) Pedagogic research: on the relative merits of the search for generalization and study of single events, *Oxford Review of Education*, 7(1): 73–93. Reproduced in Chapter 7 (omitting his appendix on pp. 88–94) in J. Bell, T. Bush, A. Fox *et al. Conducting Small-scale Investigations in Educational Management*. London: Harper and Row, in association with The Open University.

Bell, J. (1999) *Doing Your Research Project: A Guide for First-time Researchers in Education and Social Science*, 3rd edn. Buckingham: Open University Press.

Blaxter, L., Hughes, C. and Tight, M. (1996) *How to Research*. Buckingham: Open University Press.

Bloom, B.S. (ed.) (1956) *The Taxonomy of Educational Objectives. Vol. 1: Cognitive Domain*. New York, NY: Mackay.

Brewer, J.D. (2000) *Ethnography*. Buckingham: Open University Press.

Bryman, A. and Cramer, D. (1994) *Quantitative Data Analysis for Social Scientists* (revised edition). London: Routledge.

Calder, J. (1996) Statistical Techniques, in R. Sapsford and V. Jupp, *Data Collection and Analysis*, pp. 226–61. London: Sage.

Cashen, P. (1982) A study of compulsory education in South Australia between 1927 and 1939. Unpublished doctoral thesis, Adelaide University.

Chan, T. (2000) Student evaluation of teaching effectiveness. Unpublished PhD thesis, University of Nottingham.

Clarke, G.M. and Cooke, D. (1992) *A Basic Course in Statistics*, 3rd edn. London: Arnold.

Cohen, L. and Holliday, M. (1982) *Statistics for Social Scientists*. London: Harper and Row.

Cohen, L. and Holliday, M. (1996) *Practical Statistics for Students*. London: Paul Chapman.

Cohen, L. and Manion, L. (1994) *Research Methods in Education*, 4th edn. London: Routledge.

Cohen, L., Manion, L. and Morrison, J. (2000) *Research Methods in Education*, 5th edn. London: Routledge Falmer.

Cramer, D. (1997) *Basic Statistics for Social Research*. London: Routledge.

Denscombe, M. (1998) *The Good Research Guide*. Buckingham: Open University Press.

Dixon, B.R., Bouma, G.D. and Atkinson, G.B.J. (1987) *A Handbook of Social Science Research: A Comprehensive and Practical Guide for Students*. New York, NY: Oxford University Press.

Fan, G. (1998) An exploratory study of final year diploma in nursing students' perceptions of their nursing education. Unpublished MEd dissertation, University of Sheffield.

Fetterman, D. (1998) *Consumer Culture and Postmodernism*. London: Sage.

Fidler, B. (1992) Telephone interviewing, reprinted as Chapter 19 in N. Bennett, R. Glatter and R. Levačić (eds) (1994) *Improving Educational Management through Consultancy*. London: Paul Chapman.

Goulding, S. (1987) Analysis and Presentation of Information, in J. Bell, *Doing Your Research Project*. Milton Keynes: Open University Press.

Gray, J. (2000) The framing of truancy: a study of non attendance as a form of social exclusion within Western Australia. Unpublished doctoral thesis, Edith Cowan University, Western Australia.

Greene, J. and D'Oliveira, M. (1982) *Learning to Use Statistical Tests in Psychology*. Buckingham: Open University Press.

Hammersley, M. (1986) *Controversies in Classroom Research*. Milton Keynes: Open University Press.

Hammersley, M. (1990) *Classroom Ethnography*. Buckingham: Open University Press.

Hart, E. and Bond, M. (1995) *Action Research for Health and Social Care: A Guide to Practitioners*. Buckingham: Open University Press.

Haywood, P. and Wragg, E.C. (1982) *Evaluating the Literature*, Rediguide 2. Nottingham: University of Nottingham School of Education.

Hinton, P.R. (1996) *Statistics Explained: A Guide for Social Science Students*. London: Routledge.

Lim, C.P. (1997) The effect of computer-based learning (CBL) in support classes on low-performance economics students. Unpublished MEd dissertation, University of Sheffield

Lutz, F.W. (1986) Ethnography: The holistic approach to understanding schooling, in M. Hammersley, (ed.) *Controversies in Classroom Research*. Milton Keynes: Open University Press.

McMillan, J.H. and Schumacher, S. (1984) *Research in Education – A Conceptual Introduction*. Boston, MA: Little, Brown.

Masterplan for IT in Singapore (2001) Can be accessed through: http://www.moe.edu.sg/iteducation/masterplan/welcome.htm

May, T. (1993) *Social Research: Issues, Methods and Process*. Buckingham: Open University Press.

Medawar, P.B. (1972) *The Hope of Progress*. London: Methuen.

Miles, M.B. and Huberman, A.M. (1994) *Qualitative Data Analysis*, 2nd edn. Thousand Oaks, CA: Sage.

Moore, D.S. (1997) *Statistics: Concepts and Controversies*, 4th edn. New York, NY: W.H. Freeman.

Moser, C.A. and Kalton, G. (1971) *Survey Methods in Social Investigation*, 2nd edn. London: Heinemann.

Nai, C. (1996) Stretching the aged workforce: a study of the barriers to continuous learning among mature workers. Unpublished dissertation submitted in part requirement for the degree of Master of Education (Training and Development) at the University of Sheffield.

Nisbet, R.E. and Ross, L. (1980) *Human Inferences: Strategies and Shortcomings of Social Judgement*. Englewood Cliffs, NJ: Prentice Hall.

Oppenheim, A.N. (1992) *Questionnaire Design, Interviewing and Attitude Measurement*. London: Pinter.

Orna, E. with Stevens, G. (1995) *Managing Information for Research*. Buckingham: Open University Press.

Punch, K.F. (1998) *Introduction to Social Research: Quantitative and Qualitative Approaches*. London: Sage.

Rose, D. and Sullivan, O. (1996) *Introducing Data Analysis for Social Scientists*, 2nd edn. Buckingham: Open University Press.

Sapsford, R. and Jupp, V. (1996) *Data Collection and Analysis*. London: Sage.

Sapsford, R. and Abbott, P. (1996) Ethics, politics and research, in R. Sapsford and V. Jupp, *Data Collection and Analysis*. London: Sage.

Schofield, W. (1996) Survey sampling, in R. Sapsford and V. Jupp, *Data Collection and Analysis*. London: Sage.

Solomon, R. and Winch, C. (1994) *Calculating and Computing for Social Science and Arts Students*. Buckingham: Open University Press.

Stoneley, H.E. (1995) The relationship of occupational therapy students' entry qualifications to their final honours degree awards. Unpublished MEd dissertation, University of Sheffield.

Straits Times (1977) $2b IT plan to revolutionise learning unveiled, April: 1.

Verma, G.K. and Beard, R.M. (1981) *What is Educational Research? Perspectives on Techniques of Research*. Aldershot: Gower.

Wilson, M. (1996) Asking questions in R. Sapsford, and V. Jupp (eds) *Data Collection and Analysis*. London: Sage.

Wolcott, H.F. (1990) *Writing up Qualitative Research*. Qualitative Research Methods Series, Vol. 20. Newbury Park, CA: Sage.

Wolcott, H.F. (1992) Posturing in qualitative inquiry, in M.D. LeConte, W.L. Millroy and J. Preissle (eds) *The Handbook of Qualitative Research in Education.* New York: Academic Press.

Youngman, M. (1978) *Statistical Strategies*, Rediguide 20. Nottingham: University of Nottingham.

INDEX

Page numbers in *italics* refer to tables, *g* denotes a glossary definition.

INTRODUCING DATA ANALYSIS FOR SOCIAL SCIENTISTS

David Rose and Oriel Sullivan

Free Data Disk Inside

This textbook is designed for social science students taking their first course in quantitative data analysis. It requires no previous knowledge of statistics or computer use, nor any mathematics beyond an elementary level. It introduces students to the principles of analysing data in simple stages, including an introduction to using computers and SPSS/PC+, the most widely used statistical package in the social sciences. The emphasis throughout is on an understanding of the underlying principles of data analysis, and on elucidating these with simple but realistic worked examples which stress the role of theory in social research and the logic of data analysis.

The first four parts of the text give students a grasp on the logic and language of social research; preparation of data and basic ideas in computing; descriptive data statistics for both single variables and bivariate analyses; and inferential statistics. The final part introduces some of the most useful multivariate techniques and discusses the problems and potential of longitudinal studies. The text comes complete with exercises and examples from the British Class Survey, and a subset of that data on a free floppy disk inside. This is an invaluable beginner's guide to students in geography; political science, sociology, social policy, management, social psychology and related disciplines.

Contents

224pp   0 335 09708 1 (Hardback)

ETHNOGRAPHY
John D. Brewer

- What is ethnography?
- To what use can ethnographic data be put?
- Who are its fiercest critics?
- Does ethnography have a future?

Ethnography is one of the principal methods of qualitative research with a long-established tradition of use in the social sciences. However, the literature on ethnography has become a battleground as ethnography is attacked from within and without the qualitative tradition. Post-modern critics effectively deny the possibility of any objective research, whilst globalization challenges the relevance of the local and the small scale.

In this book you will be presented with a robust defence of ethnography and its continued relevance in the social sciences. The author sets out the competing methodological bases of ethnography and details its different uses as a research method. You will find guidelines for good practice in the research process, as well as advice on the analysis, interpretation and presentation of ethnographic data.

Ethnography is written as a textbook with many features to help the learning process. However, its contents are research led, informed by the author's own extensive experience of undertaking ethnographic research in dangerous and sensitive locations in Northern Ireland and elsewhere. It is a lively and engaging read on an essential topic.

Contents
Introduction – What is ethnography? – Ethnography as method and methodology – The research process in ethnography – The analysis, interpretation and presentation of ethnographic data – Uses of ethnography – Conclusion: whither ethnography? – Glossary – Bibliography – Index.

224pp   0 335 20268 3 (Paperback)   0 335 20269 1 (Hardback)